"These nineteenth- and early-twentieth-century biographies, now republished by Chelsea House, reveal an unsuspected significance. Not only are a good many of them substantively valuable (and by no means entirely superseded), but they also evoke a sense of the period, an intimacy with the attitudes and assumptions of their times."

—Professor Daniel Aaron

MUCH do they wrong our Henry wise and kind,
Morose who name thee, cynical to men,
Forsaking manners civil and refined
To build thyself in Walden woods a den, —
Then flout society, flatter the rude hind.
We better knew thee, loyal citizen!
Thou, friendship's all-adventuring pioneer,
Civility itself wouldst civilize:
Whilst braggart boors, wavering 'twixt rage and fear,
Slave hearths lay waste, and Indian huts surprise,
And swift the Martyr's gibbet would uprear:
Thou hail'dst him great whose valorous emprise
Orion's blazing belt dimmed in the sky, —
Then bowed thy unrepining head to die.

A. BRONSON ALCOTT.

CONCORD, *January, 1882.*

Henry D. Thoreau.

Other titles in this Chelsea House series:

LOUISA MAY ALCOTT, *Ednah D. Cheney*
AUDUBON AND HIS JOURNALS, *Maria R. Audubon*
HENRY WARD BEECHER, *Lyman Abbott*
WILLIAM CULLEN BRYANT, *John Bigelow*
JAMES FENIMORE COOPER, *Thomas R. Lounsbury*
RICHARD HENRY DANA, *Charles Francis Adams, Jr.*
RALPH WALDO EMERSON, *Oliver Wendell Holmes*
BENJAMIN FRANKLIN, *John Bach McMaster*
HENRY GEORGE, *Henry George, Jr.*
HORACE GREELEY, *W. A. Linn*
NATHANIEL HAWTHORNE, *George E. Woodberry*
O. HENRY, *C. Alphonso Smith*
OLIVER WENDELL HOLMES, *John T. Morse, Jr.*
WASHINGTON IRVING, *Charles Dudley Warner*
JAMES RUSSELL LOWELL AND HIS FRIENDS, *Edward Everett Hale*
COTTON MATHER, *Barrett Wendell*
THOMAS NAST, *Albert Bigelow Paine*
MARGARET FULLER OSSOLI, *Thomas Wentworth Higginson*
THOMAS PAINE, *Moncure D. Conway*
EDGAR ALLAN POE, *George E. Woodberry*
MARK TWAIN, *Albert Bigelow Paine*
NOAH WEBSTER, *Horace E. Scudder*
WALT WHITMAN, *Bliss Perry*
JOHN PETER ZENGER, *Livingston Rutherfurd*

HENRY DAVID THOREAU

FRANK B. SANBORN

INTRODUCTION BY

LEO MARX

American Men and Women of Letters Series

GENERAL EDITOR

PROFESSOR DANIEL AARON

HARVARD UNIVERSITY

CHELSEA HOUSE

NEW YORK, LONDON

1980

Cover design by Stephen O. Saxe

Printed and bound in the United States of America

Library of Congress Cataloging in Publication Data

Sanborn, Franklin Benjamin, 1831-1917.
Henry David Thoreau.

(American men and women of letters)
Reprint of the 1882 ed. published by Houghton Mifflin, Boston under title: Henry D. Thoreau, in series: American men of letters.
1. Thoreau, Henry David, 1817-1862. 2. Authors, American--19th century--Biography. I. Series II. Series: American men of letters.
PS3053.S4 1980 818'.309 [B] 80-23945
ISBN 0-87754-155-8

Chelsea House Publishers
Harold Steinberg, Chairman & Publisher
Andrew E. Norman, President
Susan Lusk, Vice President
A Division of Chelsea House Educational Communications, Inc.
70 West 40 Street, New York 10018

CONTENTS

CHAPTER IX.

CHAPTER X.

CHAPTER XI.

CHAPTER XII.

CHAPTER XIII.

General Introduction

THE VISITABLE PAST

Daniel Aaron

THE TWENTY-FIVE BIOGRAPHIES of American worthies reissued in this Chelsea House series restore an all but forgotten chapter in the annals of American literary culture. Some of the authors of these volumes—journalists, scholars, writers, professional men—would be considered amateurs by today's standards, but they enjoyed certain advantages not open to their modern counterparts. In some cases they were blood relations or old friends of the men and women they wrote about, or at least near enough to them in time to catch the contemporary essence often missing in the more carefully researched and authoritative later studies of the same figures. Their leisurely, impressionistic accounts—sometimes as interesting for what is omitted as for what is emphasized—reveal a good deal about late Victorian assumptions, cultural and social, and about the vicissitudes of literary reputation.

Each volume in the series is introduced by a

recognized scholar who was encouraged to write an idiosyncratic appraisal of the biographer and his work. The introductions vary in emphasis and point of view, for the biographies are not of equal quality, nor are the writers memorialized equally appealing. Yet a kind of consensus is discernible in these random assessments: surprise at the insights still to be found in ostensibly unscientific and old-fashioned works; in some instances admiration for the solidity and liveliness of the biographer's prose and quality of mind; respect for the pioneer historians among them who made excellent use of the limited material at their disposal.

The volumes in this American Men and Women of Letters series contain none of the startling "private" and "personal" episodes modern readers have come to expect in biography, but they illuminate what Henry James called the "visitable past." As such, they are of particular value to all students of American cultural and intellectual history.

Cambridge, Massachusetts
Spring, 1980

INTRODUCTION
TO THE
CHELSEA HOUSE EDITION

Leo Marx

One day in January, 1855, when Frank (Franklin Benjamin) Sanborn was a senior at Harvard, Henry Thoreau dropped by his room in the Yard. It seems that the *Harvard Magazine*, a college monthly of which Sanborn was an editor, had just appeared with a laudatory review of *A Week on the Concord and Merrimac Rivers* (1849) and *Walden* (1854), and the grateful author was delivering a message for the reviewer. Although Sanborn, to his disappointment, was out at the time, he used the occasion to write a letter to Thoreau introducing himself and asking permission to call upon him. On the advice of Emerson, to whom he also had made himself known, Sanborn already had decided to live in Concord, and when he moved there six weeks later he rented rooms in William Ellery Channing's house just across the way from Thoreau's. In spite of the fourteen-year age difference between them, Sanborn and Thoreau soon became friends; they saw a lot of each other in the seven remaining years of Thoreau's life, and they were brought especially close by their joint effort on behalf of John Brown and the antislavery cause. It is Sanborn's firsthand knowledge that lends the present work, published twenty years after Thoreau's death, its chief merit.

In his letter to Thoreau young Sanborn had identified himself as one of those "who at Cambridge look to Concord as a Mecca." This was not polite hyperbole. Although he had grown up on a remote New Hampshire farm, Sanborn evidently had a strong affinity for the "Concord philosophy" (Emersonian idealism), and in later life he hardly could recall a time when he had been unfamiliar with Emerson's ideas. By 1852, when he entered Harvard as a sophomore, the slavery crisis was taking dominion over New England intellectual life. Even a writer as disengaged as Emerson no longer found it possible to stand aside. The Fugitive Slave Law, which enjoined every citizen to share in the odious task of recapturing escaped blacks, must have been one of the best devices ever contrived for turning contemplative spirits into political activists. While Sanborn was at Harvard a mood of defiance to authority swept through literary Boston and Concord. Theodore Parker, whose church Sanborn attended regularly, was known to preach with a loaded revolver on his pulpit. In 1857, when John Brown came to Boston, Sanborn heard him and was captivated. He became Brown's New England agent, and it was in Sanborn's house in Concord that Thoreau first met the abolitionist martyr. The fervent social idealism of those exciting days on the eve of the Civil War left a lasting imprint on

Sanborn. Remaining in Concord, he made a life as a journalist, philanthropist, and writer whose specialty was to be retrospective studies of the literary culture to which he had been introduced in the 1850s. He wrote books about several of the leading figures of what he precociously called "the American Renaissance": Brown, Alcott, Hawthorne, Emerson and Thoreau.

Sanborn's *Thoreau* is a casual piece of writing that will not bear comparison with the minutely documented, encyclopedic biographies now being written by professional literary scholars. Like other volumes in the American Men of Letters series, this "biography" is much closer to the nineteenth-century genre of the informal biographical memoir: a loosely ordered gathering of whatever materials happen to have come easily to the gatherer's hand. The memoir, a kind of impressionistic compendium of a life and work, was offered without deference to the scholarly virtues of accuracy, detachment or completeness; nor did it generally aim at deep psychological explanation or definitive critical judgment. Often, as in the case of this memoirlike biography, it was written by someone—a friend or relative—with a privileged, undisguisedly biased view of the subject. The idea of writing an unimpeachably accurate biography probably had not occurred to Sanborn, but in any event he manifestly went about his work without feeling any need to do extensive preliminary "research" or to substantiate the admittedly "obscure anecdotes" he retails. We may assume that he began with his ideas about Thoreau clearly in mind, and simply arranged the pertinent reminiscences, anecdotes, and illustrative excerpts from college essays, letters, journals and printed works in a rough topical-chronological sequence. There is something refreshingly unself-conscious about the whole procedure, and the result is an unpretentious, easygoing book with most of the predictable flaws and virtues of its relaxed amateurishness.

We read Sanborn's *Thoreau* today

chiefly because he had lived among the literary Concordians as an impressionable young man. It would be foolish at this late date to rely upon the book as a sufficient source of biographical knowledge or psychological insight. For those purposes we now have, among other scholarly works, Walter Harding's authoritative biography, *The Days of Henry Thoreau,* and Richard Lebeaux's Eriksonian study, *Young Man Thoreau.* But neither book has that intangible authority of direct experience conveyed by Sanborn. Even though he fails to give us anything like a vivid, circumstantial account of, say, his frequent excursions with Thoreau, or dinnertime in the Thoreau household (he tells us that he dined there almost daily for two years), the fact of his closeness to the man nevertheless comes through in many ways, some of them indirect or merely tacit. Indeed, what Sanborn fails to say—the long-established clichés and banalities his memory fails to corroborate—is an instructive and refreshing feature of the book. Every literal-minded reader who takes the *Walden* self-portrait at face value would profit from having to compare that heroic image with Sanborn's quotidian account. The point is not that he gives us the unvarnished truth, but that he provides so little evidentiary support for any of the familiar stereotypical Thoreaus: the hermetic visionary seeker; the scientist manqué; the feckless "captain of a huckleberry party," precursor of the Beats and Hippies, lent credence by Emerson in the funeral sermon. The man with whom Sanborn sat at the dinner table seems not to have been any of these characters.

The contrast with Emerson's Thoreau is particularly revealing. In the eulogy, which he had published soon after the funeral as a "biographical sketch," Emerson in effect had corroborated the *Walden* self-image. This beguiling character is an odd, unaspiring Yankee nature-lover, a carefree saunterer for whom the spirit—the life—is all, the work incidental. Readers of *Walden* are told nothing about the long daily stint of the hero's real-life model at his writing table. Emerson's notion was that his young friend had missed his true calling, one of the mechanic arts, but that he fortunately had managed, somehow, to compose a good many arresting sentences and paragraphs. What this portrait leaves out, of course, is any hint of the unremitting ascetic zeal with which Thoreau actually pursued his literary vocation, and it is on this score, above all, that Sanborn's biography provides an invaluable corrective.

Sanborn's Thoreau is a writer first and last. As a Harvard sophomore he already is spinning a fantasy about "a machine . . . which would instantaneously arrange upon paper each idea as it occurs to us, without any exertion upon our part." Lacking such a contrivance, he recommends as next best the habit of "keeping a journal or record of our thoughts, feelings, studies and daily experience." It is worth noting that he wrote this college theme some three years before he began (supposedly at Emerson's suggestion) to keep his own journal. Sanborn was the first biographer who had access to Thoreau's Harvard themes, and he made good use of them in his account of the early shaping of Thoreau's distinctive literary bent. Thus we find the young writer, in a paper on "Simplicity of Style," affirming his belief in the art of communicating the "most sublime and noblest precepts . . . in a plain and simple strain."

Sanborn's Thoreau is a writer who lives among writers. Concord, Massachusetts, the farming village where he was born, and to which he returned after Harvard, surely was the community with the greatest per capita concentration of highbrow intellectuals and writers in North America. (Some were permanent, others part-time residents or frequent visitors.) On the streets of Concord, Henry Thoreau was likely to encounter one of the Alcotts or the Peabody sisters, Ellery Channing or Margaret Fuller, Emerson or Hawthorne. Writing about Hawthorne in the English Men of Letters series, Henry James retrospectively describes the New England culture of this period as intolerably dry and impoverished. But Frank Sanborn, arriving on the scene just as the first, most vigorous phase of the Transcendental movement was ending, tries to convey something of the contagious atmosphere of "strange faiths and singular apocalypses" in which young Thoreau found himself. He imagines it to have been inspiriting, and it admittedly arouses in him a certain chauvinistic excess (he compares the era with nothing less than "the age of Pericles, or of the Medici, or of Queen Elizabeth"), but at least he does place Thoreau where he belongs, in the midst of a remarkable literary ferment. Unlike many latter-day Thoreauvians, he understands the way this passionate seeker channeled his energies into "the trade and mystery of writing."

Sanborn is less successful in elucidating Thoreau's involvement in the mystery of writing than in the trade. To be sure, he is clear about the extent to which "a certain inward tendency of high Calvinism" contributed, along with European romanticism, to "the mystical part of Concord philosophy." If he does not say so explicitly, he suggests that the need back of Thoreau's unappeasable "thirst for final and concentrated expression" is essentially religious or metaphysical. That he recognizes the combined religious-literary purpose of the *Walden* experiment is evident. Thoreau, he says, "aspired to live and study and practice, so that he could write—to use his own words—'sentences which suggest far more than they say, which have an atmosphere about them, which do not report an old, but make a new impression.'" Sanborn is under no illusion about Thoreau's meaning when he tells us that his reason for going to Walden was to "transact some private business with the fewest obstacles." Unlike Emerson's always-ready captain of huckleberry parties, Sanborn's friend "lived a life of labor and study in his hut." Since he understood Thoreau's literary purposes so well, Sanborn's failure to discuss (or even mention) the unitary coherence and power of *Walden* may seem difficult to explain. But then we must remind ourselves that he was writing at a time before anyone had had much to say on that subject.

In Chapter IX, "Horace in the Role of Maecenas," Sanborn helpfully describes Thoreau as a mundane literary tradesman. In view of the way academic critics tend nowadays to abstract the classic American writers from their actual times and places, it is useful to recall how close this purest of writers came to working in Grub Street. In the 1840s Horace Greeley (the Horace of Sanborn's chapter title) voluntarily took on the role of Thoreau's patron, mentor and New York literary agent. By generous quotation from Greeley's letters to Thoreau, Sanborn shows us a seldom-mentioned aspect of this writer's life. Like many another struggling literary fellow, Thoreau felt himself to be—no doubt was—poorly treated by various publishers and editors. He is impatient to learn about the fate of manuscripts he has submitted, and impatient, too, about getting paid for work in print. Greeley's letters are filled with monetary detail, complicated accounts of bargaining with editors about the price of Thoreau's work, and at one point, incredibly enough, he feels compelled to remind Thoreau about the difficulty of serving both God and Mammon. The trouble, says Greeley, is that Thoreau's work is "too solidly good" to be profitable. "In my poor judgment, if anything is calculated to make a scoundrel of an honest man, writing to sell is that very particular thing."

But it is doubtful whether even the unillusioned Sanborn believed that Thoreau needed such advice. The subject of this casual biography is a wholeheartedly committed writer or, in the traditional sense, a poet. He may be a naturalist by habit or a moralist by constitution, but he is quintessentially a poet, says Sanborn, "by force of that shaping and controlling imagination" which is his strongest, most precious faculty.

> The character of poet is so high and so rare, in any modern civilization, and specially in our American career of nationality, that it behooves us to mark and claim all our true poets, before they are classified under some other name,—as philosophers, naturalists, romancers, or historians. Thus Emerson is primarily and chiefly a poet, and only a philosopher in his second intention; and thus also Thoreau . . .

Sanborn's belief in the rarity of the poet's symbolizing power, its inestimable worth as a collective resource, forms the moral center of this modest and engaging book.

Cambridge, Massachusetts
June, 1980

HENRY D. THOREAU.

CHAPTER I.

BIRTH AND FAMILY.

THERE died in a city of Maine, on the river Penobscot, late in the year 1881, the last member of a family which had been planted in New England a little more than a hundred years before, by a young tradesman from the English island of Jersey, and had here produced one of the most characteristic American and New English men of genius whom the world has yet seen. This lady, Miss Maria Thoreau, was the last child of John Thoreau, the son of Philip Thoreau and his wife, Marie le Galais, who, a hundred years ago, lived in the parish of St. Helier, in Jersey. This John Thoreau was born in that parish, and baptized there in the Anglican church, in April, 1754; he emigrated to New England about 1773, and in 1781 married in Boston Miss Jane Burns, the daughter of a Scotchman of some estate in the neighborhood of Stirling Castle, who had emigrated earlier to Massachusetts, and had here married Sarah Orrok, the daughter of David Orrok, a Massachusetts Quaker. Jane (Burns) Thoreau, the granddaughter of David Orrok, and the grandmother of Henry David Thoreau, died in Boston, in 1796, at the age of forty-two. Her husband, John Thoreau, Sr., removed from Boston to Concord, in 1800, lived in a house on the village square, and died there in 1801. His mother, Marie le Galais, outlived him a few weeks, dying at St. Helier, in 1801. Maria Thoreau, granddaughter and namesake of Marie le Galais, died in December, 1881, in Bangor, Maine.

From the recollections of this "aunt Maria," who outlived all her American relatives by the name of Thoreau, Henry Thoreau derived what information he possessed concerning his Jersey ancestors. In his journal for April 21, 1855, he makes this entry:—

"Aunt Maria has put into my hands to-day for safe-keeping three letters from Peter Thoreau (her uncle), directed to 'Miss Elizabeth Thoreau, Concord, near Boston,' and dated at Jersey, respectively, July 1, 1801, April 22, 1804, and April 11, 1806; also a '*Vue de la ville de St. Helier*,' accompanying the first letter. The first is in answer to one from my aunt Elizabeth, announcing the death of her father (my grandfather). He states that his mother (Marie (le Galais) Thoreau) died June 26, 1801, the day before he received aunt Elizabeth's letter, though not till after he had heard from another source of the death of his brother, which was not communicated to his mother. 'She was in the seventy-ninth year of her age,' he says, 'and retained her memory to the last. She lived with my two sisters, who took the greatest care of her.' He says that he had written to my grandfather about his oldest brother (who died about a year before), but had got no answer,—had written that he left his children, two sons and a daughter, in a good way: 'The eldest son and daughter are both married and have children; the youngest is about eighteen. I am still a widower. Of four children I have but two left,—Betsey and Peter; James and Nancy are both at rest.' He adds that he sends 'a view of our native town.'

"The second of these letters is sent by the hand of Captain John Harvey, of Boston, then at Guernsey. On the 4th of February, 1804, he had sent aunt Elizabeth a copy of the last letter he had written (which was in answer to her second), since he feared she had not received it. He says that they are still at war with the French; that they received the day before a letter from her 'uncle and aunt Le Cappelain of London;' complains of not receiving letters, and says, 'Your aunts, Betsey and Peter join with me,' etc. According to the third letter (April 11, 1806), he had received by Capt. Tonzel an answer to that he sent by Capt. Harvey, and will forward this by the former, who is going *via* Newfoundland to Boston. 'He expects to go there every year; several vessels from Jersey go there every year.' His nephew had told him, some time before, that he met a gentleman from Boston, who told him he saw the sign 'Thoreau and Hayse' there, and he therefore thinks the children must have kept up the name of the firm. 'Your cousin John is a lieutenant in the British service; he has already been in a campaign on the Continent; he is very fond of it.' Aunt Maria thinks the correspondence ceased at Peter's death, because he was the one who wrote English."

These memoranda indicate that the grandfather of Henry Thoreau was the younger son of a family of some substance in Jersey, which had a branch in London and a grandson in the army that fought under Wellington against Napoleon; that the American Thoreau engaged in trade in Boston, with a partner, and carried on business successfully for years; and that there was the same pleasant family feeling in the English and French Thoreaus that we shall see in their American descendants. Miss Maria Thoreau, in answer to a letter of mine, some years ago, sent me the following particulars of her ancestry, some of which repeat what is above stated by her nephew: —

"BANGOR, *March* 18, 1878.

"MR. SANBORN.

"*Dear Sir*, — In answer to your letter, I regret that I cannot find more to communicate. I have no earlier record of my grandparents, Philippe Thoreau and Marie Le Gallais, than a certificate of their baptism in St. Helier, Jersey, written on parchment in the year 1773. I do not know what their vocation was. My Father was born in St. Helier in April, 1754, and was married to Jane Burns in Boston, in 1781. She died in that city in the year 1796, aged forty-two years. My sister Elizabeth continued my Father's correspondence with his brother, Uncle Peter Thoreau, at St. Helier, for a number of years after Father's decease, and in one of his letters he speaks of the death of grandmother, Marie Le Gallais, as taken place so near the time intelligence reach'd them of Father's death, in 1801, it was not communicated to her. Father removed to Concord in 1800, and died there, of consumption. I do not know at what time he emigrated to this country, but have been told he was shipwreck'd on the passage, and suffered much. I think he must have left a large family circle, as Uncle Peter in his letters refers to aunts and cousins, two of which, aunts Le Cappelain and Pinkney, resided in London, and a cousin, John Thoreau, was an officer in the British army.

"Soon after Father's arrival in Boston, probably, he open'd a store on Long Wharf, as documents addressed to 'John Thoreau, merchant,' appear to signify, and one subsequently purchased 'on King Street, afterward called State Street.' And now I will remark in passing that Henry's father was bred to the mercantile line, and continued in it till failure in business; when he resorted to pencil-making, and succeeded so well as to obtain the first medal at the Salem Mechanics' Fair. I think Henry could hardly compete with his father in pencil-making, any more than he, with his peculiar genius and habits, would have been willing to spend much time in such 'craft.' His father left no will, but a competency, at least, to his family, and what was done relative to the business after his death was accomplished by his daughter Sophia. I mention this to rectify Mr. Page's mistake relating to Henry.

"And now, as I have written all I can glean of Father's family, I will turn to the maternal side, of which it appears, in religious belief, they were of the Quaker persuasion. But I was sorry to see, by good old great-great-grandfather Tillet's will, that slavery was tolerated in those days in the good State of Massachusetts, and handed down from generation to generation. My great-grandmother (Tillet) married David Orrok; her daughter, Sarah Orrok, married Mr. Burns, a Scotch gentleman. At what time he came to this country, or married, I cannot ascertain, but have often been told, to gain the consent to it of grandmother's Quaker parents, he was obliged to doff his rich apparel of gems and ruffles, and conform to the more simple garb of his Quaker bride. On a visit to his home in Scotland he died, in what year is not mentioned. Before my father's decease, a letter was received from the executor of grandfather's estate, dated Stirling, informing him there was property left to Jane Burns, his daughter in America, 'well worth coming after.' But Father was too much out of health to attend to the getting it; and the letter, subsequently put into a lawyer's hands by Brother, then the only heir, was lost.

"It has been said I inherit more of the traits of my foreign ancestry than any of my family, — which pleases me. Probably the vivacity of the French and the superstition of the Scotch may somewhat characterize me, — which it is to be hop'd the experience of an octogenarian may suitably modify. But this is nothing, here nor there. And now that I have written all that is necessary, and perhaps more, I will close, with kind wishes for health and happiness. Yours respectfully, MARIA THOREAU."

It would be hard to compress more family history into a short letter, and yet leave it so sprightly in style as this. Of the four children of Maria Thoreau's brother John and Cynthia Dunbar, — John, Helen, Henry, and Sophia, — the two eldest, John and Helen, were said to be "clear Thoreau," and the others, Henry and Sophia, "clear Dunbar;" though in fact the Thoreau traits were marked in Henry also. Let us see, then, who and what were the family of Henry Thoreau's mother, Cynthia Dunbar, who was born in Keene, N. H., in 1787. She was the daughter of Rev. Asa Dunbar, who was born at Bridgewater, Mass., in 1745; graduated at Harvard College in 1767 (a classmate of Sir Thomas Bernard and Increase Sumner); preached for a while at Bedford, near Concord, in 1769, when he was "a young candidate, newly begun to preach;" settled in Salem in 1772; resigned his pastorate in 1779; and removed to Keene just at the close of the Revolution, where he became a lawyer, and died, a little upwards of forty-two, in 1787. He married before 1776, Miss Mary Jones, the daughter of Col. Elisha Jones, of Weston, a man of wealth and influence in his town, who died in 1775. Mrs. Mary (Jones) Dunbar long outlived the husband of her youth; in middle life she married a Concord farmer, Jonas Minott, whom she also outlived; and it was in his house that her famous grandson was born in July, 1817. Mrs. Minott was left a widow for the second time in 1813, when she was sixty-five years old, and in 1815 she sent a petition to the Grand Lodge of Masons in Massachusetts, which was drawn up and indorsed by her pastor, Dr. Ripley, of Concord, and which contains a short sketch of Henry Thoreau's maternal grandfather, from whom he is said to have inherited many qualities. Mrs. Minott's petition sets forth "that her first husband, Asa Dunbar, Esq., late of Keene, N. H., was a native of Massachusetts; that he was for a number of years settled in the gospel ministry at Salem; that afterwards he was a counselor-at-law; that he was Master of a Lodge of Free and Accepted Masons at Keene, where he died; that in the cause of Masonry he was interested and active; that through some defection or misfortune of that Lodge *she* has suffered loss, both on account of what was due to him and to her, at whose house they held their meetings; that in the settlement of the estate of her late husband, Jonas Minott, Esq., late of Concord, she has been peculiarly unfortunate, and become very much straitened in the means of living comfortably; that being thus reduced, and feeling the weight of cares, of years, and of widowhood to be very heavy, after having seen better days, she is induced, by the advice of friends, as well as her own exigencies, to apply for aid to the benevolence and charity of the Masonic fraternity." At the house of this decayed gentlewoman, about two years after the date of this petition, Henry Thoreau was born. She lived to see him running about, a sprightly boy, and he remembered her with affection. One of his earliest recollections of Concord was of driving in a chaise with his grandmother along the shore of Walden Pond, perhaps on the way to visit her relatives in Weston, and thinking, as he said afterward, that he should like to live there.

Ellery Channing, whose life of his friend Henry is a mine of curious information on a thousand topics, relevant and irrelevant, and who often traversed the "old Virginia road" with Thoreau before the house in which he was born was removed from its green knoll to a spot further east, where it now stands, thus pictures the brown farm-house and its surroundings: "It was a perfect piece of our old New England style of building, with its gray, unpainted boards, its grassy, unfenced door-yard. The house is somewhat isolate and remote from thoroughfares; on the Virginia road, an old-fashioned, winding, at length deserted pathway, the more smiling for its forked orchards, tumbling walls, and mossy banks. About it are pleasant sunny meadows, deep with their beds of peat, so cheering with its homely, hearth-like fragrance; and in front runs a constant stream through the centre of that great tract sometimes called 'Bedford levels,'—the brook a source of the Shawsheen River." (This is a branch of the Merrimac, as Concord River is, but flows into the main stream through Andover, and not through Billerica and Lowell, as the Concord does.) The road on which it stands, a mile and a half east of the Fitchburg railroad station, and perhaps a mile from Thoreau's grave in the village cemetery, is a by-path from Concord to Lexington, through the little town of Bedford. The farm-house, with its fields and orchard, was a part of Mrs. Minott's "widow's thirds," on which she was living at the date of her grandson's birth (July 12, 1817), and which her son-in-law, John Thoreau, was "carrying on" for her that year.

Mrs. Minott, a few years before Dr. Ripley's petition in her behalf, came near having a more distinguished son-in-law, Daniel Webster, who, like the young Dunbars, was New Hampshire born, and a year or two older than Mrs. Minott's daughter, Louisa Dunbar. He had passed through Dartmouth College a little in love with two or three of the young ladies of Hanover, and had returned to his native town of Salisbury, N. H., when he met in Boscawen, near by, Miss Louisa, who, like Miss Grace Fletcher, whom he married a few years afterward, was teaching school in one of the New Hampshire towns. Miss Dunbar made an impression on Webster's heart, always susceptible, and, had the fates been propitious, he might have called Henry Thoreau nephew in after years; but the silken tie was broken before it was fairly knit. I suspect that she was the person referred to by one of Webster's biographers, who says, speaking of an incident that occurred in January, 1805: "Mr. Webster, at that time, had no thought of marrying; he had not even met the lady who afterward became his wife. He had been somewhat interested in another lady, who is occasionally referred to in his letters, written after he left college, but who was not either of those whom he had known at Hanover. But this affair never proceeded very far, and he had entirely dismissed it from his mind before he went to Boston in 1804." In January, 1806, about the time of his father's death, Webster wrote to a college friend, "I am not married, and seriously am inclined to think I never shall be," though he was then a humble suitor to Grace Fletcher.

Louisa Dunbar was a lively, dark-haired, large-eyed, pleasing young lady, who had perhaps been educated in part at Boscawen, where Webster studied for college, and afterwards was a school-teacher there. She received from him those attentions which young men give to young ladies without any very active thoughts of marriage; but he at one time paid special attentions to her, which might have led to matrimony, perhaps, if Webster had not soon after fallen under the sway of a more fascinating school-teacher, Miss Grace Fletcher, of Hopkinton, N. H., whom he first saw at the door of her little school-house in Salisbury, not far from his own birthplace. A Concord matron, a neighbor and friend of the

Dunbars and Thoreaus, heard the romantic story from Webster's own lips forty years afterward, as she was driving with him through the valley of the Assabet: how he was traveling along a New Hampshire road in 1805, stopped at a school-house to ask a question or leave a message, and was met at the door by that vision of beauty and sweetness, Grace Fletcher herself, to whom he yielded his heart at once. From a letter of Webster's to this Concord friend (Mrs. Louisa Cheney) I quote this description of his native region, which has never been printed: —

"FRANKLIN, N. H., *September* 29, '45.

"DEAR MRS. CHENEY, — You are hardly expecting to hear from me in this remote region of the earth. Where I am was originally a part of Salisbury, the place of my birth; and, having continued to own my father's farm, I sometimes make a visit to this region. The house is on the west bank of Merrimac River, fifteen miles above Concord (N. H.), in a pleasant valley, made rather large by a turn in the stream, and surrounded by high and wooded hills. I came here five or six days ago, alone, to try the effect of the mountain air upon my health.

"This is a very picturesque country. The hills

are high, numerous, and irregular, — some with wooded summits, and some with rocky heads as white as snow. I went into a pasture of mine last week, lying high up on one of the hills, and had there a clear view of the White Mountains in the northeast, and of Ascutney, in Vermont, back of Windsor, in the west; while within these extreme points was a visible scene of mountains and dales, lakes and streams, farms and forests. I really think this region is the true Switzerland of the United States.

"I am attracted to this particular spot by very strong feelings. It is the scene of my early years; and it is thought, and I believe truly, that these scenes come back upon us with renewed interest and more strength of feeling as we find years running over us. White stones, visible from the window, and close by, mark the grave of my father, my mother, one brother, and three sisters. Here are the same fields, the same hills, the same beautiful river, as in the days of my childhood. The human beings which knew them now know them no more. Few are left with whom I shared either toil or amusement in the days of youth. But this is melancholy and personal, and enough of it. One mind cannot enter fully into the feelings of another in regard to the past, whether those feelings be joyous or melancholy, or, which is more commonly the case, partly both. I am, dear Mrs. Cheney, yours truly, DANIEL WEBSTER."

No doubt the old statesman was thinking, as he wrote, not only of his father, Captain Ebenezer Webster ("with a complexion," said Stark, under whom he fought at Bennington, "that burnt gunpowder could not change"), of his mother and his brethren, but also of Grace Fletcher,—and echoing in his heart the verse of Wordsworth:—

> "Among thy mountains did I feel
> The joy of my desire;
> And she I cherished turned her wheel
> Beside a cottage fire.
> Thy mornings showed, thy nights concealed,
> The bowers where Lucy played;
> And thine, too, is the last green field
> That Lucy's eyes surveyed."

It was no such deep sentiment as this which Louisa Dunbar had inspired in young Webster's breast; but he walked and talked with her, took her to drive in his chaise up and down the New Hampshire hills, and no doubt went with her to church and to prayer-meeting. She once surprised me by confiding to me (as we were talking about Webster in the room where Henry Thoreau afterwards died, and where there hung then an engraving by Rowse of Webster's magnificent head) "that she regarded Mr. Webster, under Providence, as the means of her conversion." Upon my asking how, she said that, in one of their drives, — perhaps in the spring of 1804, — he had spoken to her so seriously and scripturally on the subject of religion that her conscience was awakened, and she soon after joined the church, of which she continued through life a devout member. Her friendship for Mr. Webster also continued, and in his visits to Concord, which were frequent from 1843 to 1849, he generally called on her, or she was invited to meet him at the house of Mr. Cheney, where, among social and political topics, Webster talked with her of the old days at Boscawen and Salisbury.

Cynthia Dunbar, the mother of Henry Thoreau, was born in Keene, N. H., in 1787, the year that her father died. Her husband, John Thoreau, who was a few months younger than herself, was born in Boston. When Henry Thoreau first visited Keene, in 1850, he made this remark: "Keene Street strikes the traveler favorably ; it is so wide, level, straight, and long. I have heard one of my relatives who was born and bred there [Louisa Dunbar, no doubt] say that you could see a chicken run across it a mile off." His mother hardly lived there long enough to notice the chickens a mile off, but she occasionally visited her native town after her marriage in 1812, and a kinswoman (Mrs. Laura Dunbar Ralston, of Washington, D. C.), now living, says, "I recollect Mrs. Thoreau as a handsome, high-spirited woman, half a head taller than her husband, accomplished, after the manner of those days, with a voice of remarkable power and sweetness in singing." She was fond of dress, and had a weakness, not uncommon in her day, for ribbons, which her austere friend, Miss Mary Emerson (aunt of R. W. Emerson), once endeavored to rebuke in a manner of her own. In 1857, when Mrs. Thoreau was seventy years old, and Miss Emerson eighty-four, the younger lady called on the elder in Concord, wearing bonnet-ribbons of a good length and of a bright color, — perhaps yellow. During the call, in which Henry Thoreau was the subject of conversation, Miss Emerson kept her eyes shut. As Mrs. Thoreau and her daughter Sophia rose to go, the little old lady said, "Perhaps you noticed, Mrs. Thoreau, that I closed my eyes during your call. I did so because I did not wish to look on the ribbons you are wearing, so unsuitable for a child of God and a person of your years."

In uttering this reproof, Miss Emerson may have had in mind the clerical father of Mrs. Thoreau, Rev. Asa Dunbar, whom she was old enough to remember. He was settled in Salem as the colleague of Rev. Thomas Barnard, after a long contest which led to the separation of the First Church there, and the formation of the Salem North Church in 1772. The parishioners of Mr. Dunbar declared their new minister "admirably qualified for a gospel preacher," and he seems to have proved himself a learned and competent minister. But his health was infirm, and this fact, as one authority says, "soon threw him into the profession of the law, which he honorably pursued for a few years at Keene." Whether he went at once to Keene on leaving Salem in 1779 does not appear, but he was practicing law there in 1783, and was also a leading Freemason. His diary for a few years of his early life — a faint foreshadowing of his grandson's copious journals — is still in existence, and indicates a gay and genial disposition, such as Mrs. Thoreau had. His only son, Charles Dunbar, who was born in February, 1780, and died in March, 1856, inherited this gaiety of heart, but also that lack of reverence and discipline which is proverbial in New England for "ministers' sons and deacons' daughters." His nephew said of him, "He was born the winter of the great snow, and he died in the winter of another great snow, — a life bounded by great snows." At the time of Henry Thoreau's birth, Mrs. Thoreau's sisters, Louisa and Sarah, and their brother Charles were living in Concord, or not far off, and there Louisa Dunbar died a few years before Mrs. Thoreau. Her brother Charles, who was two years older than Daniel Webster, was a person widely known in New Hampshire and Massachusetts, and much celebrated by Thoreau in his journals. At the time of his death, I find the following curious entries, in Thoreau's journal for April 3, 1856: —

"People are talking about my uncle Charles. George Minott [a sort of cousin of the Thoreaus] tells how he heard Tilly Brown once asking him to show him a peculiar inside lock in wrestling. 'Now, don't hurt me, — don't throw me hard.' He struck his antagonist inside his knees with his feet, and so deprived him of his legs. Edmund Hosmer remembers his tricks in the bar-room, shuffling cards, etc.; he could do anything with cards, yet he did not gamble. He would toss up his hat, twirling it over and over, and catch it on his head invariably. He once wanted to live at Hosmer's, but the latter was afraid of him. 'Can't we study up something?' he asked. Hosmer asked him into the house, and brought out apples and cider, and uncle Charles talked. 'You!' said he, 'I burst the bully of Haverhill.' He wanted to wrestle, — would not be put off. 'Well, we won't wrestle in the house.' So they went out to the yard, and a crowd got round. 'Come, spread some straw here,' said uncle Charles, — 'I don't want to hurt him.' He threw him at once. They tried again; he told them to spread more straw, and he 'burst' him. Uncle Charles used to say that he had n't a single tooth in his head. The fact was they were all double, and I have heard that he lost about all of them by the time he was twenty-one. Ever since I knew him he could swallow his nose. He had a strong head, and never got drunk; would drink gin sometimes, but not to excess. Did not use tobacco, except snuff out of another's box, sometimes; was very neat in his person; was not profane, though vulgar."

This was the uncle who, as Thoreau said in "Walden," "goes to sleep shaving himself, and is obliged to sprout potatoes in a cellar Sundays in order to keep awake and keep the Sabbath." He was a humorous, ne'er-do-weel character, who, with a little property, no family, and no special regard for his reputation, used to move about from place to place, a privileged jester, athlete, and unprofessional juggler. One of his tricks was to swallow all the knives and forks and some of the plates at the tavern table, and then offer to restore them if the landlord would forgive him the bill. I remember this worthy in his old age, an amusing guest at his brother-in-law's table, where his nephew plied him with questions. We shall find him mentioned again, in connection with Daniel Webster's friendship for the Dunbar family.

Thoreau's mother had this same incessant and rather malicious liveliness that in Charles Dunbar took the grotesque form above hinted at. She was a kindly, shrewd woman, with traditions of gentility and sentiments of generosity, but with sharp and sudden flashes of gossip and malice, which never quite amounted to ill-nature, but greatly provoked the prim and commonplace respectability that she so often came in contact with. Along with this humorous quality there went also an affectionate earnestness in her relation with those who depended on her, that could not fail to be respected by all who knew the hard conditions that New England life, even in a favored village like Concord, then imposed on the mother of a family, where the outward circumstances were not in keeping with the inward aspiration.

"Who sings the praise of woman in our clime?
I do not boast her beauty or her grace:
Some humble duties render her sublime,
She, the sweet nurse of this New England race,
The flower upon the country's sterile face;
The mother of New England's sons, the pride
Of every house where those good sons abide."

Her husband was a grave and silent, but inwardly cheerful and social person, who found no difficulty in giving his wife the lead in all affairs. The small estate he inherited from his father, the first John Thoreau, was lost in trade, or by some youthful indiscretions, of which he had his quiet share; and he then, about 1823, turned his attention to pencil-making, which had by that time become a lucrative business in Concord. He had married in 1812, and he died in 1859. He was a small, deaf, and unobtrusive man, plainly clad, and "minding his own business;" very much in contrast with his wife, who was one of the most unceasing talkers ever seen in Concord. Her gift in speech was proverbial, and wherever she was the conversation fell largely to her share. She fully verified the Oriental legend, which accounts for the greater loquacity of women by the fact that nine baskets of talk were let down from heaven to Adam and Eve in their garden, and that Eve glided forward first and secured six of them. Old Dr. Ripley, a few years before his death, wrote a letter to his son, towards the end of which he said, with courteous reticence, "I meant to have filled a page with sentiments. But *a kind neighbor*, Mrs. Thoreau, has been here more than an hour. This letter must go in the mail to-day." Her conversation generally put a stop to other occupations; and when at her table Henry Thoreau's grave talk with others was interrupted by this flow of speech at the other end of the board, he would pause, and wait with entire and courteous silence, until the interruption ceased, and then take up the thread of his own discourse where he had dropped it; bowing to his mother, but without a word of comment on what she had said.

Dr. Ripley was the minister of Concord for half a century, and in his copious manuscripts, still preserved, are records concerning his parishioners of every conceivable kind. He carefully kept even the smallest scrap that he ever wrote, and among his papers I once found a fragment, on one side of which was written a pious meditation, and on the other a certificate to this effect: "Understanding that Mr. John Thoreau, now of Chelmsford, is going into business in that place, and is about to apply for license to retail ardent spirits, I hereby certify that I have been long acquainted with him, that he has sustained a good character, and now view him as a man of integrity, accustomed to store-keeping, and of correct morals." There is no date, but the time was about 1818. Chelmsford is a town ten miles north of Concord, to which John Thoreau had removed for three years, in the infancy of Henry. From Chelmsford he went to Boston in 1821, but was successful in neither place, and soon returned to Concord, where he gave up trade and engaged in pencil-making, as already mentioned.

From that time, about 1823, till his death in 1859, John Thoreau led a plodding, unambitious, and respectable life in Concord village, educating his children, associating with his neighbors on those terms of equality for which Concord is famous, and keeping clear, in a great degree, of the quarrels, social and political, that agitated the village. Mrs. Thoreau, on the other hand, with her sister Louisa and her sisters-in-law, Sarah, Maria, and Jane Thoreau, took their share in the village bickerings. In 1826, when Dr. Lyman Beecher, then of

Boston, Dr. John Todd, then of Groton, and other Calvinistic divines succeeded in making a schism in Dr. Ripley's parish, and drawing off Trinitarians enough to found a separate church, the Thoreaus generally seceded, along with good old Deacon White, whose loss Dr. Ripley bewailed. This contention was sharply maintained for years, and was followed by the antimasonic and antislavery agitation. In the latter Mrs. Thoreau and her family engaged zealously, and their house remained for years headquarters for the early abolitionists and a place of refuge for fugitive slaves. The atmosphere of earnest purpose, which pervaded the great movement for the emancipation of the slaves, gave to the Thoreau family an elevation of character which was ever afterward perceptible, and imparted an air of dignity to the trivial details of life. By this time, too, — I speak of the years from 1836 onward till the outbreak of the civil war, — the children of Mrs. Thoreau had reached an age and an education which made them noteworthy persons. Helen, the oldest child, born in 1812, was an accomplished teacher. John, the elder son, born in 1814, was one of those lovely and sunny natures which infuse affection in all who come within their range; and Henry, with his peculiar strength and independence of soul, was a marked personage among the few who would give themselves the trouble to understand him. Sophia, the youngest child, born in 1819, had, along with her mother's lively and dramatic turn, a touch of art; and all of them, whatever their accidental position for the time, were superior persons. Living in a town where the ancient forms survived in daily collision or in friendly contact with the new ideas that began to make headway in New England about 1830, the Thoreaus had peculiar opportunities, above their apparent fortunes, but not beyond their easy reach of capacity, for meeting on equal terms the advancing spirit of the period.

The children of the house, as they grew up, all became school-teachers, and each displayed peculiar gifts in that profession. But they were all something more than teachers, and becoming enlisted early in the antislavery cause, or in that broader service of humanity which "plain living and high thinking" imply, they gradually withdrew from that occupation, — declining the opportunities by which other young persons, situated as they then were, rise to worldly success, and devoting themselves, within limits somewhat narrow, to the pursuit of lofty ideals. The household of which they were loving and thoughtful members (let one be permitted to say who was for a time domesticated there) had, like the best families everywhere, a distinct and individual existence, in which each person counted for something, and was not a mere drop in the broad water-level that American society tends more and more to become. To meet one of the Thoreaus was not the same as to encounter any other person who might happen to cross your path. Life to them was something more than a parade of pretensions, a conflict of ambitions, or an incessant scramble for the common objects of desire. They were fond of climbing to the hill-top, and could look with a broader and kindlier vision than most of us on the commotions of the plain and the mists of the valley. Without wealth, or power, or social prominence, they still held a rank of their own, in scrupulous independence, and with qualities that put condescension out of the question. They could have applied to themselves, individually, and without hauteur, the motto of the French chevalier:—

"Je suis ni roi, ni prince aussi,
Je suis le seigneur de Coucy."

"Nor king, nor duke? Your pardon, no;
I am the master of Thoreau."

They lived their life according to their genius, without the fear of man or of "the world's dread laugh," saying to Fortune what Tennyson sings:—

"Turn, Fortune, turn thy wheel with smile or frown,—
With that wild wheel we go not up nor down;
Our hoard is little, but our hearts are great.
Smile, and we smile, the lords of many lands;
Frown, and we smile, the lords of our own hands,—
For man is man, and master of his fate."

CHAPTER II.

CHILDHOOD AND YOUTH.

CONCORD, the Massachusetts town in which Thoreau was born, is to be distinguished from the newer but larger town of the same name which became the capital of New Hampshire about the time the first American Thoreau made his appearance in "old Concord." The latter, the first inland plantation of the Massachusetts Colony, was bought of the Indians by Major Willard, a Kentish man, and Rev. Peter Bulkeley, a Puritan clergyman from the banks of the Ouse in Bedfordshire, and was settled under their direction in 1635. Mr. Bulkeley, from whom Mr. Emerson and many of the other Concord citizens of Thoreau's day were descended, was the first minister of the town, which then included the present towns of Concord, Acton, Bedford, Carlisle, and Lincoln; and among his parishioners were the ancestors of the principal families that now inhabit these towns. Concord itself, the centre of this large tract, was thought eligible for settlement because of its great meadows on the Musketaquid or Meadow River. It had been a seat of the Massachusetts Indians, and a powerful Sachem, Tahattawan, lived between its two rivers, where the Assabet falls into the slow-gliding Musketaquid. Thoreau, the best topographer of his birthplace, says:—

"It has been proposed that the town should adopt for its coat of arms a field verdant, with the Concord circling nine times round. I have read that a descent of an eighth of an inch in a mile is sufficient to produce a flow. Our river has probably very near the smallest allowance. But wherever it makes a sudden bend it is shallower and swifter, and asserts its title to be called a river. For the most part it creeps through broad meadows, adorned with scattered oaks, where the cranberry is found in abundance, covering the ground like a mossbed. A row of sunken dwarf willows borders the stream on one or both sides, while at a greater distance the meadow is skirted with maples, alders, and other fluviatile trees, overrun with the grape-vine, which bears fruit in its season, purple, red, white, and other grapes."

From these river-grapes, by seedling cultivation, a Concord gardener, in Thoreau's manhood, bred and developed the Concord grape, which is now more extensively grown throughout the United States than any other vine, and which adorns, in vineyards large and small, the hillsides over which Thoreau rambled. The uplands are sandy in many places, gravelly and rocky in others, and nearly half the township is now covered, as it has always been, with woods of oak, pine, chestnut, and maple. It is a town of husbandmen, chiefly, with a few mechanics, merchants, and professional men in its villages; a quiet region, favorable to thought, to rambling, and to leisure, as well as to that ceaseless industry by which New England lives and thrives. Its population now approaches 4,000, but at Thoreau's birth it did not exceed 2,000. There are few great estates in it, and little poverty; the mode of life has generally been plain and simple, and was so in Thoreau's time even more than now. When he was born, and for some years afterward, there was but one church, and the limits of the parish and the township were the same. At that time it was one of the two shire towns of the great county of Middlesex, — Cambridge, thirteen miles away, being the other. It was therefore a seat of justice and a local centre of trade, — attracting lawyers and merchants to its public square much more than of late years.

Trade in Concord then was very different from what it has been since the railroad began to work its revolutions. In the old days, long lines of teams from the upper country, New Hampshire and Vermont, loaded with the farm products of the interior, stopped nightly at the taverns, especially in the winter, bound for the Boston market, whence they returned with a cargo for their own country. If a thaw came on, or there was bad sleighing in Boston, the drivers, anxious to lighten their loads, would sell and buy in the Concord public square, to the great profit of the numerous traders, whose little shops stood around or near it. Then, too, the hitching-posts in front of the shops had full rows of wagons and chaises from the neighboring towns fastened there all day long; while the owners looked over goods, priced, chaffered, and beat down by the hour together the calicoes, sheetings, shirtings, kerseymeres, and other articles of domestic need, — bringing in, also, the product of their own farms and looms to sell or exchange. Each "store" kept an assortment of "West India goods," dry goods, hardware, medicines, furniture, boots and shoes, paints, lumber, lime, and the miscellaneous articles of which the village or the farms might have need; not to mention a special trade in New England rum and old Jamaica, hogsheads of which were brought up every week from Boston by teams, and sold or given away by the glass, with an ungrudging hand. A little earlier than the period now mentioned, when Colonel Whiting (father of the late eminent lawyer, Abraham Lincoln's right-hand adviser in the law of emancipation, William Whiting, of Boston) was a lad in Concord village, "there were five stores and three taverns in the middle of the town, where intoxicating liquors were sold by the glass to any and every body; and it was the custom, when a person bought even so little as fifty cents' worth of goods, to offer him a glass of liquor, and it was generally accepted." Such was the town when John Thoreau, the Jerseyman, came there to die in 1800, and such it remained during the mercantile days of John Thoreau, his son, who was brought up in a house on the public square, and learned the business of buying and selling in the store of Deacon White, close by. Pencil-making, the art by which he earned his modest livelihood during Henry Thoreau's youth, was introduced into Concord about 1812 by William Munroe, whose son has within ten years richly endowed the small free library from which Thoreau drew books, and to which he gave some of his own. In this handicraft, which was at times quite profitable, the younger Thoreaus assisted their father from time to time, and Henry acquired great skill in it; even to the extent, says Mr. Emerson, of making as good a pencil as the best English ones. "His friends congratulated him that he had now opened his way to fortune. But he replied that he should never make another pencil. 'Why should I? I would not do again what I have done once.'" Thoreau may have said this, but he afterward changed his mind, for he went on many years, at intervals, working at his father's business, which in time grew to be mainly the preparation of fine-ground plumbago for electrotyping. This he supplied to various publishers, and among others to the Harpers, for several years. But what he did in this way was incidental, and as an aid to his father, his mother, or his sister Sophia, who herself carried on the business for some time after the death of Henry in 1862. It was the family employment, and must be pursued by somebody.

Perpetuity, indeed, and hereditary transmission of everything that by nature and good sense can be inherited, are among the characteristics of Concord. The Heywood family has been resident in Concord for two hundred and thirty years or so, and in that time has held the office of town clerk, in lineal succession from father to son, for one hundred years at least. The grandson of the first John Heywood filled the office (which is the most responsible in town, and generally accompanied by other official trusts) for eighteen years, beginning in 1731; his son held the place with a slight interregnum for thirteen years; his nephew,

Dr. Abiel Heywood, was town clerk from 1796 to 1834 without a break, and Dr. Heywood's son, Mr. George Heywood, has now been clerk for twenty-nine years, or ever since 1853.

Of the dozen ministers who, since 1635, have preached in the parish church, five were either Bulkeleys or Emersons, descendants of the first minister, or else connected by marriage with that clerical line; and the young minister who is this year (1882) to take the pastorate of Rev. Peter Bulkeley, is a descendant, and bears the same name. Mr. Emerson himself, the great clerk of Concord, which has been his lay parish for half a century since he ceased to preach in its pulpit, counts among his ancestors four of the Concord pastors, whose united ministry covered a century; while his grandmother's second husband, Dr. Ripley, added a half century more to the family ministry. For this ancestral claim, quite as much as for his gift of wit and eloquence, Mr. Emerson was chosen, in 1835, to commemorate by an oration the two hundredth aniversary of the town settlement. In this discourse he said: —

"I have had much opportunity of access to anecdotes of families, and I believe this town to have been the dwelling-place, in all times since its planting, of pious and excellent persons, who walked meekly through the paths of common life, who served God and loved man, and never let go their hope of immortality. I find our annals marked with a uniform good sense. I find no ridiculous laws, no eavesdropping legislators, no hanging of witches, no ghosts, no whipping of Quakers, no unnatural crimes. The old town clerks did not spell very correctly, but they contrived to make pretty intelligible the will of a free and just community."

Into such a community Henry Thoreau, a free and just man, was born. Dr. Heywood, above-named, was the first town clerk he remembered, and the one who entered on the records the marriage of his father and mother, and the birth of all the children. He cried the banns of John Thoreau and Cynthia Dunbar in the parish meeting-house; and he was the last clerk who made this Sunday outcry.

He thus proclaimed his own autumnal nuptials in 1822, when he married for the first time at the age of sixty-three. The banns were cried at the opening of the service, and this compelled the town clerk to be a more regular attendant in the meeting-house than his successors have found necessary. Dr. Heywood's pew was about half-way down the broad aisle, and in full view of the whole congregation, whether in the "floor pews" or "up in the galleries." Wearing his old-fashioned coat and small-clothes, the doctor would rise in his pew, deliberately adjust his spectacles, and look about for a moment, in order to make sure that his audience was prepared; then he made his proclamation with much emphasis of voice and dignity of manner. There was a distinction, however, in the manner of "publishing the banns" of the white and the black citizens; the former being "cried" in the face of the whole congregation, and the latter simply "posted" in the meeting-house porch, as was afterwards the custom for all. Dr. Heywood, from a sense of justice, or some other proper motive, determined on one occasion to "post" a white couple, instead of giving them the full benefit of his sonorous voice; but, either because they missed the *éclat* of the usual proclamation, or else felt humiliated at being "posted like niggers in the porch," they brought the town clerk to justice forthwith, and he was forced for once to yield to popular outcry, and join in the outcry himself. After publishing his own banns, and just before the wedding, he for the first time procured a pair of trousers, — having worn knee-breeches up to that time, as Colonel May (the father-in-law of Mr. Alcott) and others had thought it proper to wear them. When Dr. Heywood told his waggish junior, 'Squire Brooks, of the purchase, and inquired how young gentlemen put their trousers on, his legal neighbor advised him that they were generally put on over the head.

Dr. Heywood survived amid "this age loose and all unlaced," as Marvell says, until 1839, having practiced medicine, more or less, in Concord for upward of forty years, and held court there as a local justice for almost as long. Dr. Isaac Hurd, who was his contemporary, practiced in Concord for fifty-four years, and in all sixty-five years; and Dr. Josiah Bartlett, who accompanied and succeeded Dr. Hurd, practiced in Concord nearly fifty-eight years· while the united medical service of himself and his father, Dr. Josiah Bartlett of Charlestown, was one hundred and two years.

Dr. Bartlett himself was one of the most familiar figures in Concord through Thoreau's life-time, and for fifteen years after. To him have been applied, with more truth, I suspect, than to "Mr. Robert Levet, a Practiser in Physic," those noble lines of Dr. Johnson on his humble friend: —

> "Well tried through many a varying year,
> See Levet to the grave descend,
> Officious, innocent, sincere,
> *Of every friendless name the friend.*"

He said more than once that for fifty years no severity of weather had kept him from visiting his distant patients, — sometimes miles away, — except once, and then the snow was piled so high that his sleigh upset every two rods; and when he unharnessed and mounted his horse, the beast, floundering through a drift, slipped him off over his crupper. He was a master of the horse, and encouraged that proud creature to do his best in speed. One of his neighbors mentioned in his hearing a former horse of Dr. Bartlett's, which was in the habit of running away. "By faith!" said the doctor (his familiar oath), "I recollect that horse; he was a fine traveler, but I have no remembrance that he ever ran away." When upwards of seventy, he was looking for a new horse. The jockey said, "Doctor, if you were not so old, I have a horse that would suit you." "Hm!" growled the doctor, "don't talk to me about *old*. Let 's see your horse;" and he bought him, and drove him for eight years. He practiced among the poor with no hope of reward, and gave them, besides, his money, his time, and his influence. One day a friend saw him receiving loads of firewood from a shiftless man to whom he had rendered gratuitous service in sickness for twenty years. "Ah, doctor! you are getting some of your back pay." "By faith! no; the fellow is poor, so I paid him for his wood, and let him go."

Dr. Bartlett did not reach Concord quite in season to assist at the birth of Henry Thoreau; but from the time his parents brought him back to his native town from Boston, in 1823, to the day of Sophia Thoreau's death, in 1876, he might have sup plied the needed medical aid to the family, and often did so. The young Henry dwelt in his first tabernacle on the Virginia road but eight months, removing then to a house on the Lexington road, not far from where Mr. Emerson afterwards established his residence, on the edge of Concord village. In the mean time he had been baptized by Dr. Ripley in the parish church, at the age of three months; and his mother boasted that he did not cry. His aunt, Sarah Thoreau, taught him to walk when he was fourteen months old, and before he was sixteen months he removed to Chelmsford, "next to the meeting-house, where they kept the powder, in the garret," as was the custom in many village churches of New England then. Coming back to Concord before he was six years old, he soon began to drive his mother's cow to pasture, barefoot, like other village boys; just as Emerson, when a boy in Boston, a dozen years before, had driven his mother's cow where now the fine streets and halls are. Thoreau, like Emerson, began to go to school in Boston, where he lived for a year or more in Pinckney Street. But he returned to Concord in 1823, and, except for short visits or long walking excursions, he never left the town again till he died, in 1862. He there went on with his studies in the village schools, and fitted for Harvard College at the "Academy," which 'Squire Hoar, Colonel Whiting, 'Squire Brooks, and other magnates of the town had established about 1820. This private school was generally very well taught, and here Thoreau himself taught for a while in after years. In his boyhood it had become a good place to study Greek, and in 1830, when perhaps Henry Thoreau was one of its pupils, Mr. Charles Emerson, visiting his friends in Concord, wrote thus of what he saw there: "Mr. George Bradford and I attended the Exhibition yesterday at the Academy. We were extremely gratified. To hear little girls saying their Greek grammar and young ladies read Xenophon was a new and very agreeable entertainment." Thoreau must have been beginning his Greek grammar about that time, for he entered college in 1833, and was then proficient in Greek. He must also have gone, as a boy, to the "Concord Lyceum," where he afterwards lectured every winter. Concord, as the home of famous lawyers and active politicians, was always a place of resort for political leaders, and Thoreau might have seen and heard there all the celebrated congressmen and governors of Massachusetts, at one time and another. He could remember the visit of Lafayette to Concord in 1824, and the semicentennial celebration of the Concord Fight in 1825. In 1830 he doubtless looked forward with expectation for the promised lecture of Edward Everett before the Lyceum, concerning which Mr. Everett wrote as follows to Dr. Ripley (November 3, 1830): —

"I am positively forbidden by my physician to come to Concord to-day. To obviate, as far as possible, the inconvenience which this failure might cause the Lyceum, I send you the lecture which I should have delivered. It is one which I have delivered twice before; but my health has prevented me from preparing another. Although *in print*, as you see, it has *not been published*. I held it back from publication to enable me, with propriety, to deliver it at Concord. Should you think it worth while to have it read to the meeting, it is at your service for that purpose; and, should this be done, I would suggest, as it is one hour and three quarters long, that some parts should be omitted. For this reason I have inclosed some passages in brackets, which can be spared without affecting the context."

It would hardly occur to a popular lecturer now to apologize because he had delivered his lecture twice before, or to send the copy forward, when he could not himself be there to read it.

Mr. Emerson began to lecture in the Concord Lyceum before 1834, when he came to reside in the town. In October of that year he wrote to Dr. Ripley, declining to give the opening lecture, but offering to speak in the course of the winter, as he did. During its first half century he lectured more than a hundred times in this Lyceum, reading there, first and last, nearly all the essays he has published, and many that have never been printed. Thoreau gave his first lecture there in April, 1838, and afterwards lectured nearly every year for more than twenty years. On one occasion, very early in his public career, when the expected lecturer of the Lyceum failed to come, as Mr. Everett had failed, but had not been thoughtful enough to send a substitute, Henry Thoreau and Mr. Alcott were pressed into the service, and spoke before the audience in duet, and with opinions extremely heretical,—both being ardent radicals and "come-outers." A few years after this (in 1845), Wendell Phillips made his first appearance before the Concord Lyceum, and spoke in a manner which Thoreau has described in print, and which led to a sharp village controversy, not yet quite forgotten on either side.

But to return to the childhood and youth of Thoreau. When he was three or four years old, at Chelmsford, on being told that he must die, as well as the men in the New England Primer, and having the joys of heaven explained to him, he said, as he came in from "coasting," that he did not want to die and go to heaven, because he could not carry his sled to so fine a place; for, he added, "the boys say it is not shod with iron, and not worth a cent." At the age of ten, says Channing, "he had the firmness of the Indian, and could repress his pathos, and had such seriousness that he was called 'judge.'" As an example of childish fortitude, it is related that he carried his pet chickens for sale to the tavern-keeper in a basket; whereupon Mr. Wesson told him to 'stop a minute,' and, in order to return the basket promptly, took the darlings out, and wrung their necks, one by one, before the boy's eyes, who wept inwardly, but did not budge. Having a knack at whittling, and being asked by a schoolmate to make him a bow and arrow, young Henry refused, not deigning to give the reason, — that he had no knife. "So through life," says Channing, "he steadily declined trying or pretending to do what he had no means to execute, yet forbore explanations." He was a sturdy and kindly playmate, whose mirthful tricks are yet remembered by those who frolicked with him, and he always abounded with domestic affection. While in college he once asked his mother what profession she would have him choose. She said, pleasantly, "You can buckle on your knapsack, dear, and roam abroad to seek your fortune;" but the thought of leaving home and forsaking Concord made the tears roll down his cheeks. Then his sister Helen, who was standing by, says Channing, "tenderly put her arm around him and kissed him, saying, 'No, Henry, you shall not go; you shall stay at home and live with us.'" And this, indeed, he did, though he made one or two efforts to seek his fortune for a time elsewhere.

His reading had been wide and constant while at school, and after he entered college at the age of sixteen. His room in Cambridge was in Hollis Hall; his instructors were such as he found there, but in rhetoric he profited much by the keen intelligence of Professor Channing, an uncle of his future friend and biographer, Ellery Channing. I think he also came in contact, while in college, with that singular poet, Jones Very, of Salem. He was by no means unsocial in college, though he did not form such abiding friendships as do many young men. He graduated in 1837. His expenses at Cambridge, which were very moderate, compared with what a poor scholar must now pay to go through college, were paid in part by his father, in part by his aunts and his elder sister, Helen, who had already begun to teach school; and for the rest he depended on his own efforts and the beneficiary funds of the college, in which he had some little share. I have understood that he received the income of the same modest endowment which had been given to William and Ralph Waldo Emerson when in college, some years before; and in other ways the generous thought of that most princely man, Waldo Emerson, was not idle in his behalf, though he knew Thoreau then only as the studious son of a townsman, who needed a friend at court. What Mr. Emerson wrote to Josiah Quincy, who was then president of Harvard College, in behalf of Henry Thoreau does not appear, except from the terms of old Quincy's reply; but we may infer it. Thoreau had the resource of school-keeping in the country towns, during the college vacation and the extra vacation that a poor scholar could claim; and this brought him, in 1835, to an acquaintance with that elder scholar, Brownson, who afterwards became a Catholic doctor of theology. He left college one winter to teach school at Canton, near Boston, where he was examined by

Rev. Orestes A. Brownson, then a Protestant minister in Canton. He studied German and boarded with Mr. Brownson while he taught the school. In 1836, he records in his journal that he "went to New York with father, peddling." In his senior year, 1836–37, he was ill for a time, and lost rank with his instructors by his indifference to the ordinary college motives for study. This fact, and also that he was a beneficiary of the college, further appears from the letter of President Quincy to Mr. Emerson, as follows: —

"CAMBRIDGE, 25*th June*, 1837.

"MY DEAR SIR, — Your view concerning Thoreau is entirely in consent with that which I entertain. His general conduct has been very satisfactory, and I was willing and desirous that whatever falling off there had been in his scholarship should be attributable to his sickness. He had, however, imbibed some notions concerning emulation and college rank which had a natural tendency to diminish his zeal, if not his exertions. His instructors were impressed with the conviction that he was indifferent, even to a degree that was faulty, and that they could not recommend him, consistent with the rule by which they are usually governed in relation to beneficiaries. I have always entertained a respect for and interest in him, and was willing to attribute any apparent neglect or indifference to his ill health rather than to wilfulness. I obtained from the instructors the authority to state all the facts to the Corporation, and submit the result to their discretion. This I did, and that body granted *twenty-five dollars*, which was within *ten*, or at most *fifteen*, dollars of any sum he would have received, had no objection been made. There is no doubt that, from some cause, an unfavorable opinion has been entertained, since his return after his sickness, of his disposition to exert himself. To what it has been owing may be doubtful. I appreciate very fully the goodness of his heart and the strictness of his moral principle; and have done as much for him as, under the circumstances, was possible. Very respectfully, your humble servant,

"JOSIAH QUINCY.

"Rev. R. W. EMERSON."

It is possible the college faculty may have had other grounds of distrust in Thoreau's case. On May 30, 1836, his classmate Peabody wrote him the following letter from Cambridge, — Thoreau being then at home, for some reason, — from which we may infer that the sober youth was not averse to such deeds as are there related: —

"The Davy Club got into a little trouble, the week before last, from the following circumstance: H. W. gave a lecture on Pyrotechny, and illustrated it with a parcel of fireworks he had prepared in the vacation. As you may imagine, there was some slight noise on the occasion. In fact, the noise was so slight that Tutor B. heard it at his room in Holworthy. This worthy boldly determined to march forth and attack the 'rioters.' Accordingly, in the midst of a grand display of rockets, etc., he stepped into the room, and, having gazed round him in silent astonishment for the space of two minutes, and hearing various cries of 'Intrusion!' 'Throw him over!' 'Saw his leg off!' 'Pull his wool!' etc., he made two or three dignified motions with his hand to gain attention, and then kindly advised us to 'retire to our respective rooms.' Strange to say, he found no one inclined to follow this good advice, and *he* accordingly thought fit to withdraw. There is, as perhaps you know, a law against keeping powder in the college buildings. The effect of Tutor B.'s intrusion was evident on the next Monday night, when H. W. and B. were invited to call and see President Quincy; and owing to the tough reasoning of Tutor B., who boldly asserted that 'powder was powder,' they were each presented with a public admonition.

"We had a miniature volcano at Webster's lecture, the other morning [this was Professor Webster, afterwards hanged for the murder of Dr. Parkman], and the odors therefrom surpassed all ever produced by Araby the Blest. Imagine to yourself all the windows and shutters of the lecture-room closed, and then conceive the delightful scent produced by the burning of nearly a bushel of sulphur, phosphoretted hydrogen, and other still more pleasant ingredients. As soon as the burning commenced, there was a general rush to the door, and a crowd collected there, running out every half minute to get a breath of fresh air, and then coming in to see the volcano. 'No noise nor nothing.' Bigelow and Dr. Bacon manufactured some 'laughing gas,' and administered it on the Delta. It was much better than that made by Webster. Jack Weiss took some, as usual; Wheeler, Jo Allen, and Hildreth each received a dose. Wheeler proceeded to dance for the amusement of the company, Jo jumped over the Delta fence, and Sam raved about Milton, Shakespeare, Byron, etc. He took two doses; it produced a great effect on him. He seemed to be as happy as a mortal could desire; talked with Shakespeare, Milton, etc., and seemed to be quite at home with them."

The persons named were classmates of Thoreau: one of them afterward Rev. John

Weiss; Wheeler was of Lincoln, and died early in Germany, whither he went to study; Samuel Tenney Hildreth was a brother of Richard Hildreth, the historian, and also died young. The zest with which his classmate related these pranks to Thoreau seems to imply in his correspondent a mind too ready towards such things to please the learned faculty of Cambridge.

Mr. Quincy's letter was in reply to one which Mr. Emerson had written at the request of Mrs. Thoreau, who feared her son was not receiving justice from the college authorities. Thoreau graduated without much distinction, but with a good name among his classmates, and a high reputation for general scholarship. When he went to Maine, in May, 1838, to see if there was not some school for him to teach there, he took with him this certificate from his pastor, Dr. Ripley:—

"CONCORD, *May* 1, 1838.

"TO THE FRIENDS OF EDUCATION,— The undersigned very cheerfully hereby introduces to public notice the bearer, Mr. David Henry Thoreau, as a teacher in the higher branches of useful literature. He is a native of this town, and a graduate of Harvard University. He is well disposed and well qualified to instruct the rising generation. His scholarship and moral character will bear the strictest scrutiny. He is modest and mild in his disposition and government, but not wanting in energy of character and fidelity in the duties of his profession. It is presumed his character and usefulness will be appreciated more highly as an acquaintance with him shall be cultivated. Cordial wishes for his success, reputation, and usefulness attend him, as an instructor and gentleman.

" EZRA RIPLEY,

"*Senior Pastor of the First Church in Concord, Mass.*

" N. B. — *It is but justice to observe here that the eyesight of the writer is much impaired.*"

Accompanying this artless document is a list of clergymen in the towns of Maine, — Portland, Belfast, Camden, Kennebunk, Castine, Ellsworth, etc., — in the handwriting of the good old pastor, signifying that as young Thoreau traveled he should report himself to these brethren, who might forward his wishes. But even at that early date, I suspect that Thoreau undervalued the " D. D.'s " in comparison with the "chickadedees," as he plainly declared in his later years. Another certificate, in a firmer hand, and showing no token of impaired eyesight, was also carried by Thoreau in this first visit to Maine. It was this: —

"I cordially recommend Mr. Henry D. Thoreau, a graduate of Harvard University in August, 1837, to the confidence of such parents or guardians as may propose to employ him as an instructor. I have the highest confidence in Mr. Thoreau's moral character, and in his intellectual ability. He is an excellent scholar, a man of energy and kindness, and I shall esteem the town fortunate that secures his services.

"R. WALDO EMERSON.

"CONCORD, *May* 2, 1838."

The acquaintance of Mr. Emerson with his young townsman had begun perhaps a year before this date, and had advanced very fast toward intimacy. It originated in this way: A lady connected with Mr. Emerson's family was visiting at Mrs. Thoreau's while Henry was in college, and the conversation turned on a lecture lately read in Concord by Mr. Emerson. Miss Helen Thoreau surprised the visitor by saying, "My brother

Henry has a passage in his diary containing the same things that Mr. Emerson has said." This remark being questioned, the diary was produced, and, sure enough, the thought of the two passages was found to be very similar. The incident being reported to Mr. Emerson, he desired the lady to bring Henry Thoreau to see him, which was soon done, and the intimacy began. It was to this same lady (Mrs. Brown, of Plymouth) that Thoreau addressed one of his earliest poems, — the verses called "Sic Vita," in the "Week on the Concord and Merrimac," commencing: —

> "I am a parcel of vain strivings, tied
> By a chance bond together."

These verses were written on a strip of paper inclosing a bunch of violets, gathered in May, 1837, and thrown in at Mrs. Brown's window by the poet-naturalist. They show that he had read George Herbert carefully, at a time when few persons did so, and in other ways they are characteristic of the writer, who was then not quite twenty years old.

It may be interesting to see what old Quincy himself said, in a certificate, about his stubbornly independent pupil. For the same Maine journey Cambridge furnished the Concord scholar with this document:—

"HARVARD UNIVERSITY, CAMBRIDGE,
March 26, 1838.

"TO WHOM IT MAY CONCERN,—I certify that Henry D. Thoreau, of Concord, in this State of Massachusetts, graduated at this seminary in August, 1837; that his rank was high as a scholar in all the branches, and his morals and general conduct unexceptionable and exemplary. He is recommended as well qualified as an instructor, for employment in any public or private school or private family. JOSIAH QUINCY,
"*President of Harvard University.*"

It seems that there was question, at this time, of a school in Alexandria, near Washington (perhaps the Theological Seminary for Episcopalians there), in which young Thoreau might find a place; for on the 12th of April, 1838, President Quincy wrote to him as follows:—

"SIR,—The school is at Alexandria; the students are said to be young men well advanced in ye knowledge of ye Latin and Greek classics; the requisitions are, qualification and *a person who has had experience in school keeping.* Salary $600 a year, besides washing and Board; duties to be entered on ye 5th or 6th of May. If you choose to apply, I will write as soon as I am informed of it. State to me your experience in school keeping. Yours,

"JOSIAH QUINCY."

We do not know that Thoreau offered himself for the place; and we know that his journey to Maine was fruitless. He did, in fact, teach the town grammar school in Concord for a few weeks in 1837, and in July, 1838, was teaching, at the Academy I think, in Concord. He had already, as we have seen, though not yet twenty-one, appeared as a lecturer before the Concord Lyceum. It is therefore time to consider him as a citizen of Concord, and to exhibit further the character of that town.

CHAPTER III.

CONCORD AND ITS FAMOUS PEOPLE.

The Thoreau family was but newly planted in Concord, to which it was alien both by the father's and the mother's side. But this wise town adopts readily the children of other communities that claim its privileges, — and to Henry Thoreau these came by birth. Of all the men of letters that have given Concord a name throughout the world, he is almost the only one who was born there. Emerson was born in Boston, Alcott in Connecticut, Hawthorne in Salem, Channing in Boston, Louisa Alcott in Germantown, and others elsewhere; but Thoreau was native to the soil. And since his genius has been shaped and guided by the personal traits of those among whom he lived, as well as by the hand of God and by the intuitive impulses of his own spirit, it is proper to see what the men of Concord have really been. It is from them we must judge the character of the town and its civilization, not from those exceptional, imported persons — cultivated men and women, — who may be regarded as at the head of society, and yet may have no representative quality at all. It is not by the few that a New England town is to be judged, but by the many. Yet there were a Few and a Many in Concord, between whom certain distinctions could be drawn, in the face of that general equality which the institutions of New England compel. Life in our new country had not yet been reduced to the ranks of modern civilization — so orderly outward, so full of mutiny within.

It is mentioned by Tacitus, in his life of Agricola, that this noble Roman lived as a child in Marseilles; "a place," he adds, "of Grecian culture and provincial frugality, mingled and well blended." I have thought this felicitous phrase of Tacitus most apposite for Concord as I have known it since 1854, and as Thoreau must have found it from 1830 onward. Its people lived then and since with little display, while learning was held in high regard; and the "plain living and high thinking," which Wordsworth declared were gone from England, have never been absent from this New England town. It has always been a town of much social equality, and yet of great social and spiritual contrasts. Most of its inhabitants have lived in a plain way for the two centuries and a half that it has been inhabited; but at all times some of them have had important connections with the great world of politics, affairs, and literature. Rev. Peter Bulkeley, the founder and first minister of the town, was a near kinsman of Oliver St. John, Cromwell's solicitor-general, of the same noble English family that, a generation or two later, produced Henry St. John, Lord Bolingbroke, the brilliant, unscrupulous friend of Pope and Swift. Another of the Concord ministers, Rev. John Whiting, was descended, through his grandmother, Elizabeth St. John, wife of Rev. Samuel Whiting, of Lynn, from this same old English family, which, in its long pedigree, counted for ancestors the Norman Conqueror of England and some of his turbulent posterity. He was, says the epitaph over him in the village burying-ground, "a gentleman of singular hospitality and generosity, who never detracted from the character of any man, and was a universal lover of mankind." In this character some representative gentleman of Concord has stood in every generation since the first settlement of the little town.

The Munroes of Lexington and Concord are descended from a Scotch soldier of Charles II.'s army, captured by Cromwell at the battle of Worcester in 1651, and allowed to go into exile in America. His powerful kinsman, General George Munro, who commanded for Charles at the battle of Worcester, was, at the Restoration, made commander-in-chief for Scotland.

Robert Cumming, father of Dr. John Cumming, a celebrated Concord physician, was one of the followers of the first Pretender in 1715, and when the Scotch rebellion of that year failed, Cumming, with some of his friends, fled to New England, and settled in Concord and the neighboring town of Stow.

Duncan Ingraham, a retired sea-captain, who had enriched himself in the Surinam trade, long lived in Concord, before and after the Revolution, and one of his grand-children was Captain Marryatt, the English novelist; another was the American naval captain, Ingraham, who brought away Martin Kosta, a Hungarian refugee, from the clutches of the Austrian government. While Duncan Ingraham was living in Concord, a hundred years ago, a lad from that town, Joseph Perry, who had gone to sea with Paul Jones, became a high naval officer in the service of Catharine of Russia, and wrote to Dr. Ripley from the Crimea in 1786 to inquire what had become of his parents in Concord, whom he had not seen or heard from for many years. The stepson of Duncan Ingraham, Tilly Merrick, of Concord, who graduated at Cambridge in 1773, made the acquaintance of Sir Archibald Campbell, when wounded in the Concord Fight, that Scotch officer having been brought to the house of Mrs. Ingraham, Merrick's mother, and there nursed until he was well. A few years later Merrick was himself captured twice on his way to and from Holland and France, whither he went as secretary or attaché to our ambassador, John Adams. The first time he was taken to London; the second time to Halifax, where, as it happened, Sir Archibald was then in command as Governor of Nova Scotia. Young Merrick went presently to the governor's quarters, but was refused admission by the sentinel, — while parleying with whom, Sir Archibald heard the conversation, and came forward. He at once recognized his Concord friend, greeted him cordially with "How do you do, my little rebel?" and after taking good care of him, in remembrance of his own experience in Concord, procured Merrick's exchange for one of Burgoyne's officers, captured at Saratoga. Returning to America after the war, Tilly Merrick went into an extensive business at Charleston, S. C., with the son of Duncan Ingraham for a partner, and there became the owner of large plantations, worked by slaves, which he afterwards lost through reverses in business. Coming back to Concord in 1798, with the remnants of his South Carolina fortune, and inheriting his mother's Concord estate, he married a lady of the Minott family, and became a country store-keeper in his native town. His daughter, Mrs. Brooks, was for many years the leader of the antislavery party in Concord, and a close friend of the Thoreaus, who at one time lived next door to her hospitable house.

Soon after Mr. Emerson fixed his home in Concord, in 1834, a new bond of connection between the town and the great world outside this happy valley began to appear, — the genius of that man whose like has not been seen in America, nor in the whole world in our century: —

"A large and generous man, who, on our moors,
Built up his thought (though with an Indian tongue,
And fittest to have sung at Persian feasts),
Yet dwelt among us as the sage he was, —
Sage of his days, — patient and proudly true;
Whose word was worth the world, whose heart was pure.
Oh, such a heart was his! no gate or bar;
The poorest wretch that ever passed his door
Welcome as highest king or fairest friend."

This genius, in one point of view so solitary, but in another so universal and social, soon made itself felt as an attractive force, and Concord became a place of pilgrimage, as it has remained for so many years since. When Theodore Parker left Divinity Hall, at Cambridge, in 1836, and began to preach in Unitarian pulpits, he fixed his hopes on Concord as a parish, chiefly because Emerson was living there. It is said that he might have been called as a colleague for Dr. Ripley, if it had not been thought his sermons were too learned for the Christians of the Nine-Acre Corner and other outlying hamlets of the town. In 1837–38 Mr. Alcott began to visit Mr. Emerson in Concord, and in 1840 he went there to live. Margaret Fuller and Elizabeth Peabody, coadjutors of Mr. Alcott in his Boston school, had already found their way to Concord, where Margaret at intervals resided, or came and went in her sibylline way. Ellery Channing, one of the nephews of Dr. Channing, the divine, took his bride, a sister of Margaret Fuller, to Concord in 1841; and Hawthorne removed thither, upon his marriage with Miss Peabody's sister Sophia, in 1842. After noticing what went on about him for a few years, in his seclusion at the Old Manse, Hawthorne thus described the attraction of Concord, in 1845:

"It was necessary to go but a little way beyond my threshold before meeting with stranger moral shapes of men than might have been encountered elsewhere in a circuit of a thousand miles. These hobgoblins of flesh and blood were attracted thither by the wide-spreading influence of a great original thinker, who had his earthly abode at the opposite extremity of our village. His mind acted upon other minds of a certain constitution with wonderful magnetism, and drew many men upon long pilgrimages to speak with him face to face. Young visionaries, to whom just so much of insight had been imparted as to make life all a labyrinth around them, came to seek the clew that should guide them out of their self-involved bewilderment. Gray-headed theorists, whose systems, at first air, had finally imprisoned them in an iron framework, traveled painfully to his door, not to ask deliverance, but to invite the free spirit into their own thralldom. People that had lighted on a new thought, or a thought that they fancied new, came to Emerson, as the finder of a glittering gem hastens to a lapidary to ascertain its quality and value."

The picture here painted still continued to be true until long after the death of Thoreau; and the attraction was increased at times by the presence in the village of Hawthorne himself, of Alcott, and of others who made Concord their home or their haunt. Thoreau also was resorted to by pilgrims, who came sometimes from long distances and at long intervals, to see and talk with him.

There was in the village, too, a consular man, for many years the first citizen of Concord, — Samuel Hoar, — who made himself known abroad by sheer force of character and "plain heroic magnitude of mind." It was of him that Emerson said, at his death in November, 1856, —

"He was a man in whom so rare a spirit of justice visibly dwelt that if one had met him in a cabin or in a forest he must still seem a public man, answering as sovereign state to sovereign state; and might easily suggest Milton's picture of John Bradshaw, that he 'was a consul from whom the fasces did not depart with the year, but in private seemed ever sitting in judgment on kings.' He returned from courts or congresses to sit down with unaltered humility, in the church or in the town-house, on the plain wooden bench, where Honor came and sat down beside him."

In his house and in a few others along the elm-planted street, you might meet at any time other persons of distinction, beauty, or wit, — such as now and then glance through the shining halls of cities, and, in great centres of the world's civilization, like London or Paris, muster

"In solemn troops and sweet societies,"

which are the ideal of poets and fair women, and the envy of all who aspire to social eminence. Thoreau knew the worth of this luxury, too, though, as a friend said of him, "a story from a fisher or hunter was better to him than an evening of triviality in shining parlors, where he was misunderstood."

There were not many such parlors in Concord, but there was and had constantly been in the town a learned and social element, such as gathers in an old New England village of some wealth and inherited culture. At the head of this circle — which fell off on one side into something like fashion and mere amusement, on another into the activity of trade or politics, and rose, among the women especially, into art and literature and religion — stood, in Thoreau's boyhood and youth, a grave figure, yet with something droll about him, — the parish minister and county Nestor, Dr. Ezra Ripley, who lived and died in the "Old Manse."

Dr. Ripley was born in 1751, in Woodstock, Conn., the same town in which Dr. Abiel Holmes, the father of the poet Holmes, was born. He entered Harvard

College in 1772, came with the students to Concord in 1775, when the college buildings at Cambridge were occupied by Washington and his army, besieging Boston, and graduated in 1776. Among his classmates were Governor Gore, Samuel Sewall, the second chief-justice of Massachusetts of that name, and Royal Tyler, the witty chief-justice of Vermont. Governor Gore used to say that in college he was called "Holy Ripley," from his devout character. He settled in Concord in 1778, and at the age of twenty-nine married the widow of his last predecessor, Rev. William Emerson (and the daughter of his next predecessor, Rev. Daniel Bliss), who was at their marriage ten years older than her husband, and had a family of five children. Dr. Ripley's own children were three in number: the Reverend Samuel Ripley, born May 11, 1783; Daniel Bliss Ripley, born August 1, 1784; and Miss Sarah Ripley, born August 8, 1789. When this daughter died, not long after her mother, in 1826, breaking, says Mr. Emerson, "the last tie of blood which bound me and my brothers to his house," Dr. Ripley said to Mr. Emerson, "I wish you and your brothers to come to this house as you have always done. You will not like to be excluded; I shall not like to be neglected." He died himself in September, 1841.

Of Dr. Ripley countless anecdotes are told in his parish, and he is the best remembered person, except Thoreau himself, who has died in Concord for a century; just as his house, described so finely by Hawthorne in his "Mosses," is still the best known house in Concord. It was for a time the home of Mr. Emerson, and there, it is said, he wrote his first book, "Nature," concerning which, when it came out anonymously, the question was asked, "Who is the author of 'Nature'?" The reply was, of course, "God and Ralph Waldo Emerson." The Old Manse was built about 1766 for Mr. Emerson's grandfather, then minister of the parish, and into it he brought his bride, Miss Phebe Bliss (daughter of Rev. Daniel Bliss, of Concord, and Phebe Walker, of Connecticut). Miss Mary Emerson, youngest child of this marriage, used to say "she was in arms at the battle of Concord," because her mother held her up, then two years old, to see the soldiers from her window; and from his study window her father saw the fight at the bridge. It was the scene of many of the anecdotes, told of Dr. Ripley, some of which, gathered from various sources, may here be given; it was also, after his death, one of the resorts of Thoreau, of Margaret Fuller, of Ellery Channing, of Dr. Hedge, and of the Transcendentalists in general. His parishioners to this day associate Dr. Ripley's form "with whatever was grave and droll in the old, cold, unpainted, uncarpeted, square-pewed meeting-house, with its four iron-gray deacons in their little box under the pulpit; with Watts's hymns; with long prayers, rich with the diction of ages; and, not less, with the report like musketry from the movable seats."[1] One of these "iron-gray deacons," Francis Jarvis, used to visit the Old Manse with his children on Sunday evenings, and his son, Dr. Edward Jarvis, thus describes another side of Dr. Ripley's pastoral character: —

[1] *Emerson's Sketch of Dr. Ripley.* Hood, in his *Music for the Million,* describes an angry man as slamming a door "with a *wooden damn.*"

"Among the very pleasant things connected with the Sabbaths in the Jarvis family were the visits to Dr. Ripley in the evening. The doctor had usually a small levee of such friends as were disposed to call. Deacon Jarvis was fond of going there, and generally took with him one of the children and his wife, when she was able. There were at these levees many of the most intelligent and agreeable men of the town,—Mr. Samuel Hoar, Mr. Nathan Brooks, Mr. John Keyes, Deacon Brown, Mr. Pritchard, Major Burr, etc. These were extremely pleasant gatherings. The little boys sat and listened, and remembered the cheerful and instructive conversation. There were discussions of religion and morals, of politics and philosophy, the affairs of the town, the news of the day, the religious and social gossip, pleasant anecdotes and witty tales. All were in their best humor. Deacon Jarvis [adds his son], did not go to these levees every Sunday night, though he would have been glad to do so, had he been less distrustful. When his children, who had no such scruples, asked him to go and take them with him, he said he feared that Dr. Ripley would not like to see him so frequently."

According to Mr. Emerson, Dr. Ripley was "a natural gentleman; no dandy, but courtly, hospitable, and public spirited; his house open to all men." An old farmer who used to travel thitherward from Maine, where Dr. Ripley had a brother settled in the ministry, used to say that "no horse from the Eastern country would go by the doctor's gate." It was one of the listeners at his Sunday evening levees, no doubt, who said (at the time when Dr. Ripley was preparing for his first and last journey to Baltimore and Washington, in the presidency of the younger Adams) "that a man who could tell a story so well was company for kings and for John Quincy Adams."

When P. M., after his release from the State Prison, had the effrontery to call on Dr. Ripley, as an old acquaintance, as they were talking together on general matters, his young colleague, Rev. Mr. Frost, came in. The doctor presently said, "Mr. M., my brother and colleague, Mr. Frost, has come to take tea with me. I regret very much the causes (very well known to you), which make it impossible for me to ask you to stay and break bread with us." Mr. Emerson, his grandson (by Dr. Ripley's marriage with the widow of Rev. William Emerson) relates that he once went to a funeral with Dr. Ripley, and heard him address the mourners. As they approached the farm-house the old minister said that the eldest son, who was now to succeed the deceased father of a family in his place as a Concord yeoman, was in some danger of becoming intemperate. In his remarks to this son, he presently said, —

"Sir, I condole with you. I knew your great-grandfather; when I came to this town, in 1778, he was a substantial farmer in this very place, a member of the church, and an excellent citizen. Your grandfather followed him, and was a virtuous man. Now your father is to be carried to his grave, full of labors and virtues. There is none of that old family left but you, and it rests with you to bear up the good name and usefulness of your ancestors. If *you* fail — Ichabod! — the glory is departed. Let us pray."

He took Mr. Emerson about with him in his chaise when a boy, and in passing each house he would tell the story of its family, dwelling especially on the nine church-members who had made a division in the church in the time of his predecessor; every one of the nine having come to bad fortune or a bad end. "The late Dr. Gardiner," says Mr. Emerson, "in a funeral sermon on some parishioner, whose virtues did not readily come to mind, honestly said, 'He was good at fires.' Dr. Ripley had many virtues, and yet, even in his old age, if the firebell was rung, he was instantly on horse-back, with his buckets and bag." He had even some willingness, perhaps not equal to the zeal of the Hindoo saint, to extinguish the Orthodox fires of hell, which had long blazed in New England,—so that men might worship God with less fear. But he had small sympathy with the Transcendentalists when they began to appear in Concord. When Mr. Emerson took his friend Mr. Alcott to see the old doctor, he gave him warning that his brilliant young kinsman was not quite sound in the faith, and bore testimony in particular against a sect of his own naming, called "Egomites" (from *ego* and *mitto*), who "sent themselves" on the Lord's errands without any due call thereto. Dr. Channing viewed the "apostles of the newness" with more favor, and could pardon something to the spirit of liberty which was strong in them. The occasional correspondence between the Concord shepherd of his people and the great Unitarian preacher is full of interest. In February, 1839, when he was eighty-eight years old and weighed down with infirmities, he could still lift up his voice in testimony. He then wrote to Dr. Channing: —

"Broken down with the infirmities of age, and subject to fits that deprive me of reason and the use of my limbs, I feel it a duty to be patient and submissive to the will of God, who is too wise to err, and too good to injure. My mind labors and is oppressed, viewing the present state of Christianity, and the various speculations, opinions, and practices of the passing period. Extremes appear to be sought and loved, and their novelty gains attention. You, sir, appear to retain and act upon the sentiment of the Latin phrase, —

"'Est modus in rebus, sunt certi denique fines.'

"The learned and estimable Norton appears to me to have weakened his hold on public opinion and confidence by his petulance or pride, his want of candor and charity."

Six years earlier, Dr. Channing had written to Dr. Ripley almost as if replying to some compliment like this, and expressed himself thus, in a letter dated January 22, 1833, —

"I thank God for the testimony which you have borne to the usefulness of my writings. Such approbation from one whom I so much venerate, and who understands so well the wants and signs of the times, is very encouraging to me. If I have done anything towards manifesting Christianity in its simple majesty and mild glory I rejoice, and I am happy to have contributed anything towards the satisfaction of your last years. It would gratify many, and would do good, if, in the quiet of your advanced age, you would look back on the eventful period through which you have passed, and would leave behind you, or give now, a record of the changes you have witnessed, and especially of the progress of liberal inquiry and rational views in religion." [1]

Dr. Ripley's prayers were precise and undoubting in their appeal for present provi-

[1] At the date of this letter Dr. Ripley was not quite eighty-two, and he lived to be more than ninety. Mr. Alcott, who has now passed the age of eighty-two, has been for years doing in some degree what Dr. Channing urged the patriarch of his denomination to do, but which the old minister never found time and strength for. It is curious that these two venerable men, whose united life in Concord covers a period of more than a century, both came from Connecticut.

dences. He prayed for rain and against the lightning, "that it may not lick up our spirits;" he blessed the Lord for exemption from sickness and insanity,—"that we have not been tossed to and fro until the dawning of the day, that we have not been a terror to ourselves and to others." One memorable occasion, in the later years of his pastorate, when he had consented to take a young colleague, is often remembered in his parish, now fifty years after its date. The town was suffering from drought, and the farmers from Barrett's Mill, Bateman's Pond, and the Nine-Acre Corner had asked the minister to pray for rain. Mr. Goodwin (the father of Professor Goodwin, of Harvard University) had omitted to do this in his morning service, and at the noon intermission Dr. Ripley was reminded of the emergency by the afflicted farmers. He told them courteously that Mr. Goodwin's garden lay on the river, and perhaps he had not noticed how parched the uplands were; but he entered the pulpit that afternoon with an air of resolution and command. Mr. Goodwin, as usual, offered to relieve the doctor of the duty of leading in prayer, but the old shepherd, as Mr. Emerson says, "rejected his offer with some humor, and with an air that said to all the congregation, 'This is no time for you young Cambridge men; the affair, sir, is getting serious; I will pray myself.'" He did so, and with unusual fervor demanded rain for the languishing corn and the dry grass of the field. As the story goes, the afternoon opened fair and hot, but before the dwellers in Nine-Acre Corner and the North Quarter reached their homes a pouring shower rewarded the gray-haired suppliant, and reminded Concord that the righteous are not forsaken. Another of Mr. Emerson's anecdotes bears on this point: —

"One August afternoon, when I was in his hayfield, helping him, with his man, to rake up his hay, I well remember his pleading, almost reproachful looks at the sky, when the thunder-gust was coming up to spoil his hay. He raked very fast, then looked at the cloud, and said, 'We are in the Lord's hand,— mind your rake, George! we are in the Lord's hand;' and seemed to say, 'You know me; this field is mine,— Dr. Ripley's, thine own servant.'"

In his later years Dr. Ripley was much

distressed by a schism in his church, which drew off to a Trinitarian congregation several of his oldest friends and parishioners. Among the younger members who thus seceded, fifty-six years ago, were the maiden aunts of Thoreau, Jane and Maria, — the last of whom, and the last of the name in America, has died recently, as already mentioned. Thoreau seceded later, but not to the "Orthodox" church, — as much against the wish of Dr. Ripley, however, as if he had. In later years, Thoreau's church (of the Sunday Walkers) was recognized in the village gossip; so that when I first spent Sunday in Concord, and asked my landlord what churches there were, he replied, "The Unitarian, the Orthodox, and the Walden Pond Association." To the latter he professed to belong, and said its services consisted in walking on Sunday in the Walden woods. Dr. Ripley would have viewed such rites with horror, but they have now become common. His Old Manse, which from 1842 to 1846 was occupied by Hawthorne, was for twenty years (1847–1867) the home of Mrs. Sarah Ripley, that sweet and learned lady, and has since been the dwelling-place of her children, the grand-children of Dr. Ripley. Near by stands now the statue of the Concord Minute-Man of 1775, marking the spot to which the Middlesex farmers came

> "In sloven dress and broken rank,"

and where they stood when in unconscious heroism they

> "Fired the shot heard round the world,"

and drove back the invading visitor from their doorsteps and cornfields.

Dr. Ripley, however, seldom repelled a visitor or an invader, unless he came from too recent an experience in the state prison, or offered to "break out" his path on a Sunday, when he had fancied himself too much snow-bound to go forth to his pulpit. The anecdote is characteristic, if not wholly authentic. One Sunday, after a severe snow-storm, his neighbor, the great farmer on Ponkawtassett Hill, half a mile to the northward of the Old Manse, turned out his ox-teams and all his men and neighbors to break a path to the meeting-house and the tavern. Wallowing through the drifts, they had got as far as Dr. Ripley's gate, while the good parson, snugly blocked in by a drift completely filling his avenue of ash-trees, thought of nothing less than of going out to preach that day. The long team of oxen, with much shouting and stammering from the red-faced farmer, was turned out of the road and headed up the avenue, when Dr. Ripley, coming to his parsonage door, and commanding silence, began to berate Captain B. for breaking the Sabbath and the roads at one stroke, — implying, if not asserting, that he did it to save time and oxen for his Monday's work. Angered at the ingratitude of his minister, the stammering farmer turned the ten yoke of cattle round in the doctor's garden, and drove on to the village, leaving the parson to shovel himself out and get to meeting the best way he could. Meanwhile, the teamsters sat in the warm bar-room at the tavern, and cheered themselves with punch, flip, grog, and toddy, instead of going to hear Dr. Ripley hold forth; and when he had returned to his parsonage they paraded their oxen and sleds back again, past his gate, with much more shouting than at first. This led to a long quarrel between minister and parishioner, in course of which, one day, as the doctor halted his chaise in front of the farmer's house on the hill, the stammering captain came forward, a peck measure in his hand, with which he had been giving his oxen their meal, and began to renew the unutterable grievance. Waxing warm, as the doctor admonished him afresh, he smote with his wooden measure on the shafts of the chaise, until his gentle wife, rushing forth, called on the neighbors to stop the fight which she fancied was going on between the charioteer of the Lord and the foot-soldier.

Despite these outbursts, and his habitual way of looking at all things "from the parochial point of view," as Emerson said of him, he was also a courteous and liberal-minded man, as the best anecdotes of him constantly prove. He was the sovereign of his people, managing the church, the schools, the society meetings, and, for a time, the Lyceum, as he thought fit. The lecturers, as well as the young candidates for school-keeping — Theodore Parker, Edward Everett, and the rest — addressed themselves to him, and when he met Webster, then the great man of Massachusetts, it was on equal terms.

Daniel Webster was never a lyceum lecturer in Concord, and he did not often try cases there, but was sometimes consulted in causes of some pecuniary magnitude. When Humphrey Barrett died (whose management of his nephew's estate will be mentioned in the next chapter), his heir by will (a young man without property, until he should inherit the large estate bequeathed him), found it necessary to employ counsel against the heirs-at-law, who sought to break the will. His attorney went to Mr. Webster in Boston and related the facts, adding that his client could not then pay a large fee, but might, if the cause were gained, as Mr. Webster thought it would be. "You may give me one hundred dollars as a retainer," said Webster, "and tell the young man, from me, that when I win his case I shall send him a bill that will make his hair stand on end." It so happened, however, that Webster was sent to the Senate, and the case was won by his partner.

In the summer of 1843, while Thoreau

was living at Staten Island, Webster visited Concord to try an important case in the county court, which then held sessions there. This was the "Wyman Trial," long famous in local traditions, Webster and Choate being both engaged in the case, and along with them Mr. Franklin Dexter and Mr. Rockwood Hoar, the latter a young lawyer, who had been practicing in the Middlesex courts for a few years, where his father, Mr. Samuel Hoar, was the leader of the bar. Judge Allen (Charles Allen of Worcester) held the court, and the eminent array of counsel just named was for the defense.

The occasion was a brilliant one, and made a great and lasting sensation in the village. Mr. Webster and his friends were entertained at the houses of the chief men of Concord, and the villagers crowded the court-house to hear the arguments and the colloquies between the counsel and the court. Webster was suffering from his usual summer annoyance, the "hay catarrh," or "rose cold," which he humorously described afterward in a letter to a friend in Concord: —

"You know enough of my miserable catarrh. Its history, since I left your hospitable roof, is not worth noting. There would be nothing found in it, either of the sublime or the beautiful; nothing fit for elegant description or a touch of sentiment. Not that it has not been a great thing in its way; for I think the *sneezing* it has occasioned has been truly transcendental. A fellow-sufferer from the same affliction, who lived in Cohasset, was asked, the other day, what in the world he took for it? His reply was that he 'took eight handkerchiefs a day.' And this, I believe, is the approved mode of treatment; though the *doses* here mentioned are too few for severe cases. Suffice it to say, my dear lady, that either from a change of air, or the progress of the season, or, what is more probable, from the natural progress of the disease itself, I am much better than when I left Concord, and I propose to return to Boston to-day, feeling, or hoping, that I may now be struck off the list of invalids."

Notwithstanding this affliction, Mr. Webster made himself agreeable to the ladies of Concord, old and young, and even the little girls, like Louisa Alcott, went to the courthouse to see and hear him. He was present at a large tea-party given by Mrs. R. W.

Emerson in his honor, and he renewed his old acquaintance with the Dunbars and Thoreaus. Mr. Emerson, writing to Thoreau September 8, 1843, said, briefly, "You will have heard of our 'Wyman Trial,' and the stir it made in the village. But the Cliff and Walden, which know something of the railroad, knew nothing of that; not a leaf nodded; not a pebble fell; — why should I speak of it to you?" Thoreau was indeed interested in it, and in the striking personality of Webster. To his mother he wrote from Staten Island (August 29, 1843): —

"I should have liked to see Daniel Webster walking about Concord; I suppose the town shook, every step he took. But I trust there were some sturdy Concordians who were not tumbled down by the jar, but represented still the upright town. Where was George Minott? he would not have gone far to see him. Uncle Charles should have been there; — he might as well have been catching cat-naps in Concord as anywhere. And, then, what a whetter-up of his memory this event would have been! You'd have had all the classmates again in alphabetical order reversed, — 'and Seth Hunt and Bob Smith — and he was a student of my father's — and where's Put now? and I wonder — you —

if Henry 's been to see George Jones yet? A little account with Stow — Balcolm — Bigelow — poor, miserable t-o-a-d (sound asleep). I vow — you — what noise was that? saving grace — and few there be. That 's clear as preaching — Easter Brooks — morally depraved — how charming is divine philosophy — some wise and some otherwise — Heighho! (Sound asleep again.) Webster 's a smart fellow — bears his age well. How old should you think he was? you — does he look as if he were two years younger than I?' "

This uncle was Charles Dunbar, of course, who was in fact two years older than Webster, and, like him, a New Hampshire man. He and his sisters — the mother and the aunt of Henry Thoreau — had known Webster in his youth, when he was a poor young lawyer in New Hampshire; and the acquaintance was kept up from time to time as the years brought them together. Whenever Webster passed a day in Concord, as he did nearly every year from 1843 to 1850, he would either call on Miss Dunbar, or she would meet him at tea in the house of Mr. Cheney, a college classmate of Mr. Emerson, whom he usually visited; and whose garden was a lovely plot, ornamented with great elm trees, on the bank of the Musketaquid. Mrs. Thoreau was often included in these friendly visits; and it was of this family, as well as of the Emersons, Hoars, and Brookses, no doubt, that Webster was thinking when he sadly wrote to Mrs. Cheney his last letter, less than a year before his death in 1852. In this note, dated at Washington, November 1, 1851, when he was Secretary of State under Fillmore, Mr. Webster said: —

"I have very much wished to see you all, and in the early part of October seriously contemplated going to Concord for a day. But I was hindered by circumstances, and partly deterred also by changes which have taken place. My valued friend, Mr. Phinney (of Lexington), is not living; and many of those whom I so highly esteemed, in your beautiful and quiet village, have become a good deal estranged, to my great grief, by abolitionism, free-soilism, transcendentalism, and other notions, which I cannot (but) regard as so many vagaries of the imagination. These former warm friends would have no pleasure, of course, in intercourse with one of old-fashioned opinions. Nevertheless, dear Mrs. Cheney, if I live to see another summer, I will make a visit to your house, and talk about former times and former things."

He never came; for in June, 1852, the Whig convention at Baltimore rejected his name as a Presidential candidate, and he went home to Marshfield to die. The tone of sadness in this note was due, in part, perhaps, to the eloquent denunciation of Webster by Mr. Emerson in a speech at Cambridge in 1851, and to the unequivocal aversion with which Webster's contemporary, the first citizen of Concord, Samuel Hoar, spoke of his 7th of March speech, and the whole policy with which Webster had identified himself in those dreary last years of his life. Mr. Hoar had been sent by his State in 1846 to protest in South Carolina against the unconstitutional imprisonment at Charleston of colored seamen from Massachusetts; and he had been driven by force from the State to which he went as an envoy. But, although Webster knew the gross indignity of the act, and introduced into his written speech in March, 1850, a denunciation of it, he did not speak this out in the Senate, nor did it appear in all the authorized editions of the speech. He could hardly expect Mr. Hoar to welcome him in Concord after he had uttered his willingness to return fugitive slaves, but forgot to claim reparation for so shameful an affront to Massachusetts as the Concord Cato had endured.

Mr. Webster was attached to Concord — as most persons are who have ever spent pleasant days there — and used to compliment his friend on his house and garden by the river side. Looking out upon his great trees from the dining-room window, he once said: "I am in the terrestrial paradise, and I will prove it to you by this. America is the finest continent on the globe, the United States the finest country in America, Massachusetts the best State in the Union, Concord the best town in Massachusetts, and my friend Cheney's field the best acre in Concord." This was an opinion so like that often expressed by Henry Thoreau, that one is struck by it. Indeed, the devotion of Thoreau to his native town was so marked as to provoke opposition. "Henry talks about Nature," said Madam Hoar (the mother of Senator Hoar, and daughter of Roger Sherman of Connecticut), "just as if she'd been born and brought up in Concord."

CHAPTER IV.

THE EMBATTLED FARMERS.

It was not the famous lawyers, the godly ministers, the wealthy citizens, nor even the learned ladies of Concord, who interested Henry Thoreau specially, — but the sturdy farmers, each on his hereditary acres, battling with the elements and enjoying that open-air life which to Thoreau was the only existence worth having. As his best biographer, Ellery Channing, says: "He came to see the inside of every farmer's house and head, his pot of beans, and mug of hard cider. Never in too much hurry for a dish of gossip, he could sit out the oldest frequenter of the bar-room, and was alive from top to toe with curiosity."

Concord, in our day, and still more in Thoreau's childhood, was dotted with frequent old farm-houses, of the ample and picturesque kind that bespeaks antiquity and hospitality. In one such he was born, though not one of the oldest or the best. He was present at the downfall of several of these ancient homesteads, in whose date and in the fortunes of their owners for successive generations, he took a deep interest; and still more in their abandoned orchards and door-yards, where the wild apple tree and the vivacious lilac still flourished.

To show what sort of men these Concord farmers were in the days when their historical shot was fired, let me give some anecdotes and particulars concerning two of the original family stocks, — the Hosmers, who first settled in Concord in 1635, with Bulkeley and Willard, the founders of the town; and the Barretts, whose first ancestor, Humphrey Barrett, came over in 1639. James Hosmer, a clothier from Hawkhurst in Kent, with his wife Ann (related to Major Simon Willard, that stout Kentishman, Indian trader and Indian fighter, who bought of the Squaw Sachem the township of Concord, six miles square), two infant daughters, and two maid-servants, came from London to Boston in the ship "Elizabeth," and the next year built a house on Concord Street, and a mill on the town brook.

From him descended James Hosmer, who was killed at Sudbury in 1658, in an Indian fight, Stephen, his great-grandson, a famous surveyor, and Joseph, his great-great-grandson, one of the promoters of the Revolution, who had a share in its first fight at Concord Bridge. Joseph Hosmer was the son of a Concord farmer, who, in 1743, seceded from the parish church, because Rev. Daniel Bliss, the pastor, had said in a sermon (as his opponents averred), "that it was as great a sin for a man to get an estate by honest labor, if he had not a single aim at the glory of God, as to get it by gaming at cards or dice." What this great-grandfather of Emerson did say, a century before the Transcendental epoch, was this, as he declared: "If husbandmen plow and sow that they may be rich, and live in the pleasures of this world, and appear grand before men, they are as far from true religion in their plowing, sowing, etc., as men are that game for the same purpose." Thomas Hosmer, being a prosperous husbandman, perhaps with a turn for display, took offense, and became a worshipper at what was called the "Black Horse Church,"—a seceding conventicle which met at the tavern with the sign of the Black Horse, near where the Concord Library now stands. Joseph Hosmer, his boy, was known at the village school as "the little black colt," — a lad of adventurous spirit, with dark eyes and light hair, whose mother, Prudence Hosmer, would repeat old English poetry until all her listeners but her son were weary. When he was thirty-nine years old, married and settled, a farmer and cabinet-maker, there was a convention in the parish church to consider the Boston Port Bill, the doings of General Gage in Boston, and the advice of Samuel Adams and John Hancock to resist oppression. Daniel Bliss, the leading lawyer and leading Tory in Concord, eldest son of Parson Bliss, and son-in-law of Colonel Murray, of Rutland, Vt., the chief Tory of that region, made a speech in this convention against the patriotic party. He was a graceful and fluent speaker, a handsome man, witty, sarcastic, and popular, but with much scorn for the plain people. He painted in effective colors the power of the mother country and the feebleness of the colonies ; he was elegantly dressed, friendly in his manner, but discouraging to the popular heart, and when he sat down, a deep gloom seemed to settle on the assembly. His brother-in-law, Parson Emerson, an ardent patriot, if present, was silent. From a corner of the meeting-house there rose at last a man with sparkling eyes, plainly dressed in butternut brown, who began to speak in reply to the handsome young Tory, at first slowly and with hesitation, but soon taking fire at his own thoughts, he spoke fluently, in a strain of natural eloquence, which gained him the ear and applause of the assembly. A delegate from Worcester, who sat near Mr. Bliss, noticed that the Tory was discomposed, biting his lip, frowning, and pounding with the heel of his silver-buckled shoe. "Who is the speaker?" he asked of Bliss. "Hosmer, a Concord mechanic," was the scornful reply. "Then how does he come by his English?" "Oh, he has an old mother at home, who sits in her chimney-corner and reads and repeats poetry all day long;" adding in a moment, "He is the most dangerous rebel in Concord, for he has all the young men at his back, and where he leads the way they will surely follow."

Four months later, in April, 1775, this Concord mechanic made good the words of his Tory townsman, for it was his speech to the minute-men which goaded them on to the fight. After forming the regiment as adjutant, he addressed them, closing with these words: "I have often heard it said that the British boasted they could march through our country, laying waste every village and neighborhood, and that we would not dare oppose them, — *and I begin to believe it is true.*" Then turning to Major Buttrick, who commanded, and looking off from the hill-side to the village, from which a thick smoke was rising, he cried, "Will you let them burn the town down?" whereupon the sturdy major, who had no such intention, ordered his men to march; and when, a few minutes later, the British fired on his column of companies, the Acton men at the head, he sprang from the ground shouting, "Fire, fellow-soldiers, for God's sake fire!" and discharged his own piece at the same instant. The story has often been told, but will bear repetition. Thoreau heard it in 1835 from the lips of Emerson, as he pronounced the centennial discourse in honor of the town's settlement and history; but he had read it and heard it a hundred times before, from his earliest childhood. Mr. Emerson added, after describing the fight:—

"These poor farmers who came up, that day, to defend their native soil, acted from the simplest instincts; they did not know it was a deed of fame they were doing. These men did not babble of glory; they never dreamed their children would contend which had done the most. They supposed they had a right to their corn and their cattle, without paying tribute to any but their own governors. And as they had no fear of man, they yet did have a fear of God. Captain Charles Miles, who was wounded in the pursuit of the enemy, told my venerable friend (Dr. Ripley), who sits by me, 'that he went to the services of that day with the same seriousness and acknowledgment of God, which he carried to church.'"

Humphrey Barrett, fifth in descent from the original settler, was born in 1752, on the farm his ancestors had owned ever since 1640, and was no doubt in arms at Concord Fight in 1775. His biographer says:—

"Some persons slightly acquainted with him in the latter part of his life, judged him to be unsocial, cold, and indifferent, but those most acquainted with him knew him to be precisely the reverse. The following acts of his life make apparent some traits of his character. A negro, by the name of Cæsar Robbins, had been in the habit of getting all the wood for his family use for many years from Mr. Barrett's wood-lot near by him; this being done with the knowledge and with the implied if not the express consent of the owner. Mr. Barrett usually got the wood for his own use from another part of his farm; but on one occasion he thought he would get it from the lot by Cæsar's. He accordingly sent two men with two teams, with directions to cut only hard wood. The men had been gone but a few hours when Cæsar came to Mr. Barrett's house, his face covered with sweat, and in great agitation, and says, 'Master Barrett, I have come to let you know that a parcel of men and teams have broke into our wood-lot, and are making terrible destruction of the very best trees, and unless we do something immediately I shall be ruined.' Mr. Barrett had no heart to resist this appeal of Cæsar's; he told him not to be alarmed, for he would see that he was not hurt, and would put the matter right. He then wrote an order to his men to cut no more wood, but to come directly home with their teams, and sent the order by Cæsar."[1]

The biographer of Mr. Barrett, who was also his attorney and legal adviser, goes on to say: —

"A favorite nephew who bore his name, and whose guardian he was, died under age in 1818, leaving a large estate, and no relatives nearer than uncle and aunt and the children of deceased aunts. Mr. Barrett believed that the estate in equity ought to be distributed equally between the uncle and aunt and the children of deceased aunts by right of representation.[2] And although advised that such was not the law, he still insisted upon having the question carried before the Supreme Court for decision;

[1] This princely anecdote is paralleled, in its way, by one told of Gershom Bradford, of Duxbury, son of Colonel Gam. Bradford, the friend of Washington and Kosciusko, but himself a plain Old Colony farmer. Once walking in his woods, he saw a man cutting down a fine tree; he concealed himself that the man might not see him, and went home. When asked why he did not stop the trespasser, he replied, "Could not the poor man have a tree?" Gershom Bradford was a descendant of Governor Bradford, the Pilgrim, and uncle of Mrs. Sarah Ripley, of Concord.

[2] This would, of course, diminish his own share, as the law then stood, from one half the estate to one fourth, or less.

and when the court decided against his opinion, he carried out his own views of equity by distributing the portion that fell to him according to his opinion of what the law ought to be. After he had been fully advised that the estate would be distributed in a manner he thought neither equitable nor just, he applied to the writer to make out his account as guardian; furnishing the evidence, as he believed, of the original amount of all his receipts as such guardian. I made the account, charging him with interest at six per cent. on all sums from the time of receipt till the time of making the account. Mr. Barrett took the account for examination, and soon returned it with directions to charge him with compound interest, saying that he believed he had realized as much as that. I accordingly made the account conform to his directions. He then wished me to present this account to the party who claimed half the estate, and ask him to examine it with care and see if anything was omitted. This was done, and no material omission discovered, and no objection made. Mr. Barrett then said that he had always kept all the property of his ward in a drawer appropriated for the purpose; that he made the amount of property in the drawer greater than the balance of the account; and (handing to me the contents of the drawer) he wished me to ascertain the precise sum to which it amounted. I found that it exceeded the balance of the account by $3,221.59. He then told me, in substance, that he was quite unwilling to have so large an amount of property go where it was in danger of being distributed inequitably, and particularly as he was confident he had disclosed every source from which he had realized any property of his ward, and also the actual amount received; *but*, as he knew not how it got into the drawer, and had intended all the property there to go to his nephew, he should not feel right to retain it, and therefore directed me to add it to the amount of the estate, — which was done." [1]

Conceive a community in which such characters were common, and imagine whether the claim of King George and the fine gentlemen about him, to tax the Americans without their own consent would be likely to succeed! I find in obscure anecdotes like this sufficient evidence that if John Hampden had emigrated to Massachusetts when he had it in mind, he would have found

[1] "These facts," says his biographer, whom I knew well, "show clearly, I think, not only that his love of right was stronger than his love of money, but that he would rather make any sacrifice of property than leave a doubt in his own mind whether justice had been done to others."

men like himself tilling their own acres in Concord. The Barretts, from their name, may have been Normans, but, like Hampden, the Hosmers were Saxons, and held land in England before William the Conqueror. When Major Hosmer, who was adjutant, and formed the line of the regiment that returned the British fire at Concord Bridge, had an estate to settle about 1785, the heir to which was supposed to be in England, he employed an agent, who was then visiting London, to notify the heir, and also desired him to go to the Heralds' Office and ascertain what coat-of-arms belonged to any branch of the Hosmer family. When the agent (who may have been Mr. Tilly Merrick, of Concord, John Adams's attaché in Holland), returned to America, after reporting his more important business to Major Hosmer, he added, —

"I called at the Heralds' Office in London, and the clerk said, '*There was no coat-of-arms for you, and, if you were an Englishman you would not want one; for* (he said) *there were Hosmers in Kent long before the Conquest; and at the battle of Hastings, the men of Kent were the vanguard of King Harold.*'"

If Major Hosmer's ancestors failed to drive back the invaders then, their descendants made good the failure in Concord seven centuries later.

Thoreau's favorite walk, as he tells us, — the pathway toward Heaven, — was along the old Marlborough road, west and southwest from Concord village, through deep woods in Concord and in Sudbury. To reach this road he passed by the great Hosmer farm-house, built by the old major already mentioned, in 1760 or thereabout, and concerning which there is a pretty legend that Thoreau may have taken with him along the Marlborough road. In 1758, young Jo. Hosmer, "the little black colt," drove to Marlborough one autumn day with a load of furniture he had made for Jonathan Barnes, a rich farmer, and town clerk in thrifty Marlborough. He had received the money for his furniture, and was standing on the doorstep, preparing to go home, when a young girl, Lucy Barnes, the daughter of the house, ran up to him and said, "Concord woods are dark, and a thunderstorm is coming up; you had better stay all night." "Since you ask me, I will," was the reply, and the visit was often repeated in the next few months. But when he asked farmer Jonathan for his daughter, the reply was, —

"Concord plains are barren soil. Lucy had better marry her cousin John, whose father will give him one of the best farms in Marlborough, with a good house on it, and Lucy can match his land acre for acre."

Joseph returned from that land of Egypt, and like a wise youth took the hint, and built a house of his own, planting the elm trees that now overshadow it, after a hundred and twenty years. After the due interval he went again to Marlborough, and found Lucy Barnes in the September sunshine, gathering St. Michael's pears in her father's garden. Cousin John was married, by this time, to another damsel. Miss Lucy was bent on having her own way and her own Joseph; and so Mr. Barnes gave his consent. They were married at Christmas, 1761; and Lucy came home behind him on his horse, through the same Concord woods. She afterwards told her youngest son, with some pique: —

"When my brother Jonathan was married, and

went to New Hampshire, twenty couples on horseback followed them to Haverhill, on the Merrimac, but when your father and I were married, we came home alone through these dark Concord woods."[1]

The son of this lively Lucy Hosmer, Rufus Hosmer, of Stow, was a classmate, at Cambridge, of Washington Allston, the late Chief Justice Shaw, and Dr. Charles Lowell, father of Lowell the poet. They graduated in 1798, and Dr. Lowell afterwards wrote: —

"I can recall with peculiar pleasure a vacation passed in Concord in my senior year, which Loammi Baldwin, Lemuel Shaw, Washington Allston, and myself spent with Rufus Hosmer at his father's house. I recall the benign face of Major Hosmer, as he stood in the door to receive us, with his handsome daughter-in-law (the wife of Capt. Cyrus Hosmer) on his arm. There was a charming circle of young people then living in Concord, and we boys enjoyed this very

[1] Lucy Barnes, daughter of Jonathan and Rachel Barnes of Marlborough, was born July 7, 1742, married Joseph Hosmer, of Concord, December 24, 1761, and died in Concord, , . Her brother was Rev. Jonathan Barnes, born in 1749, graduated at Harvard College, in 1770, and settled as a minister in Hillsborough, N. H., where he died in 1805.

much; but we liked best of all to stay at home and listen to the Major's stories. It was very pleasant to have a rainy day come for this, and hard to tell which seemed the happier, he or we."

Forty years afterward, in 1838, Dr. Lowell's son, James Russell Lowell, coming under college discipline, was sent to Concord to spend a similar summer vacation, and wrote his class poem in that town.

Major Hosmer died in 1821, at the age of eighty-five. Mr. Samuel Hoar, long the leader of the Middlesex County bar, who knew him in his later life, once said,—

"In two respects he excelled any one I have ever known; he was more entirely free from prejudice, and also the best reader of men. So clear was his mind and so strong his reasoning power, that I would have defied the most eloquent pleader at the bar to have puzzled him, no matter how skillfully he concealed the weak points of the case. I can imagine him listening quietly, and saying in his slow way, 'It's a pity so many fine words should be wasted, for, you see, the man's on the wrong side.'"

Another old lawyer of Concord, who first saw Major Hosmer when he was a child of ten, and the Major was sixty years old, said,—

"I then formed an opinion of him in two respects that I never altered: First, that he had the handsomest eyes I ever saw; second, those eyes saw the inside of my head as clearly as they did the outside."

He was for many years sheriff of the county, and it was the habit of the young lawyers in term-time to get round his chair and ask his opinion about their cases. Such was his knowledge of the common law, and so well did he know the judges and jurymen, that when he said to Mr. Hoar, "I fear you will lose your case," that gentleman said, "from that moment I felt it lost, for I never knew him to make a wrong guess." He was a Federalist of the old school, and in his eyes Alexander Hamilton was the first man in America. His son held much the same opinion of Daniel Webster.

Near by Major Hosmer's farm-house stood the old homestead and extensive farm buildings of the Lee family, who at the beginning of the Revolution owned one of the two or three great farms in Concord. This estate has been owned and sold in one parcel of about four hundred acres ever since it was first occupied by Henry Woodhouse about 1650. It lies between the two rivers Assabet and Musketaquid, and includes Nahshawtuc, or Lee's Hill, on which, in early days, was an Indian village. The Lees inherited it from the original owner, and held it for more than one hundred years, though it narrowly escaped confiscation in 1775, its owner being a Tory. Early in the present century it fell, by means of a mortgage, into the hands of "old Billy Gray" (the founder of the fortunes that for two or three generations have been held in the Gray family of Boston), was by him sold to Judge Fay, of Cambridge, and by him, in 1822, conveyed to his brother-in-law, Joseph Barrett, of Concord, a distant cousin of the Humphrey Barrett, mentioned elsewhere. Joseph Barrett had been one of Major Hosmer's deputies, when the old yeoman was sheriff, but now turned his attention to farming his many acres, and deserves mention here as one of the Concord farmers of two generations after the battle, among whom Henry Thoreau grew up. Indeed, the Lee Farm was one of his most accustomed haunts, since the river flowed round it for a mile or two, and its commanding hill-top gave a prospect toward the western and north-western mountains, Wachusett and Monadnoc chief among the beautiful brotherhood, whom Thoreau early saluted with a dithyrambic verse: —

> "With frontier strength ye stand your ground,
> With grand content ye circle round,
> (Tumultuous silence for all sound),
> Ye distant nursery of rills,
> Monadnoc and the Peterboro hills;
> . . . .
> But special I remember thee,
> Wachusett, who, like me,
> Standest alone without society;
> Thy far blue eye
> A remnant of the sky."

Lee's Hill (which must be distinguished from Lee's Cliff, three miles further up the main river), was the centre of this farm, and almost of the township itself, and Squire Barrett, while he tilled its broad acres (or left them untilled), might be called the centre of the farmers of his county. He was for some years president of the Middlesex Agricultural Society (before which, in later years, Emerson, and Thoreau, and Agassiz gave addresses), and took the prize in the plowing-match at its October cattle-show, holding his own plow, and driving his oxen himself. Descending from the committee-room in dress coat and ruffled shirt, he found his plow-team waiting for him, but his rivals in the match already turning their furrows. Laying off his coat, and fortifying himself with a pinch of maccaboy, while, as his teamster vowed, "that nigh-ox had his eye on the 'Squire from the time he hove in sight, ready to start the minute he took the plow-handles,"—then stepping to the task, six feet and one inch in height, and in weight two hundred and fifty pounds, the 'Squire began, and before the field was plowed he had won the premium. He was one of the many New England yeomen we have all known, who gave the lie to the common saying about the sturdier bulk and sinew of our beer-drinking cousins across the water. 'Squire Barrett could lift a barrel of cider into a cart, and once carried on his shoulders, up two flights of stairs, a sack containing eight bushels of Indian corn, which must have weighed more than four hundred pounds. He was a good horseman, an accomplished dancer, and in the hayfield excelled in the graceful sweep of his scythe and the flourish of his pitchfork.

In course of time (1840) Mr. Alcott, with his wife (a daughter of Colonel May, of Boston), and those daughters who have since become celebrated, came to live in the Hosmer cottage not far from 'Squire Barrett's, and under the very eaves of Major Hosmer's farm-house, to which in 1761 came the fair and willful Lucy Barnes. The portly and courtly 'Squire, who knew Colonel May, came to call on his neighbors, and had many a chat with Mrs. Alcott about her Boston kindred, the Mays, Sewalls, Salisburys, etc. His civility was duly returned by Mrs. Alcott, who, when 'Squire Barrett was a candidate for State Treasurer in 1845, was able, by letters to her friends in Boston, to give him useful support. He was chosen, and held the office till his death in 1849, when Thoreau had just withdrawn from his Walden hermitage, and was publishing his first book, "A Week on the Concord and Merrimack."

Thoreau's special friend among the farmers was another character, Edmund Hosmer, a scion of the same prolific Hosmer stock, who died in 1881. Edmund Hosmer, with Mr. Alcott, George Curtis and his brother Burrill, and other friends, helped Thoreau raise the timbers of his cabin in 1845, and was often his Sunday visitor in the hermitage. Of him it is that mention is made in "Walden," as follows: —

"On a Sunday afternoon, if I chanced to be at home, I heard the crunching of the snow, made by the step of a long-headed farmer, who from far through the woods sought my house, to have a social 'crack;' one of the few of his vocation who are 'men on their farms;' who donned a frock instead of a professor's gown, and is as ready to extract the moral out of church or state as to haul a load of manure from his barn-yard. We talked of rude and simple times, when men sat about large fires in cold, bracing weather, with clear heads; and when other dessert failed, we tried our teeth on many a nut which wise squirrels have long since abandoned, — for those which have the thickest shells are commonly empty."

Edmund Hosmer, who was a friend of Mr. Emerson also, and of whom George Curtis and his brother hired land which they cultivated for a time, has been celebrated in prose and verse by other Concord authors. I suppose it was he of whom Emerson wrote thus in his apologue of Saadi, many years ago: —

"Said Saadi, — When I stood before
Hassan the camel-driver's door,
I scorned the fame of Timour brave, —
Timour to Hassan was a slave.
In every glance of Hassan's eye
I read rich years of victory.
And I, who cower mean and small
In the frequent interval
When wisdom not with me resides,
Worship Toil's wisdom that abides.
I shunned his eyes — the faithful man's,
I shunned the toiling Hassan's glance."

Edmund Hosmer was also, in George Curtis's description of a conversation at Mr. Emerson's house in 1845, "the sturdy farmer neighbor, who had bravely fought his way through inherited embarrassments to the small success of a New England husbandman, and whose faithful wife had seven times merited well of her country." And it may be that he was Ellery Channing's

"Spicy farming sage,
Twisted with heat and cold and cramped with age,
Who grunts at all the sunlight through the year,
And springs from bed each morning with a cheer.

Of all his neighbors he can something tell,
'T is bad, whate'er, we know, and like it well!
The bluebird's song he hears the first in spring, —
Shoots the last goose bound south on freezing wing."

Hosmer might have sat, also, for the more idyllic picture of the Concord farmer, which Channing has drawn in his "New England": —

"This man takes pleasure o'er the crackling fire,
His glittering axe subdued the monarch oak;
He earned the cheerful blaze by something higher
Than pensioned blows. — he owned the tree he stroke,
And knows the value of the distant smoke,
When he returns at night, his labor done,
Matched in his action with the long day's sun."

Near the small farm of Edmund Hosmer, when Mr. Curtis lived with him and sometimes worked on his well-tilled acres, lay a larger farm, which, about the beginning of Thoreau's active life, was brought from neglect and barrenness into high cultivation by Captain Abel Moore, another Concord farmer, and one of the first, in this part of the country, to appreciate the value of our bog-meadows for cultivation by ditching and top-dressing with the sand which Nature had so thoughtfully ridged up in hills close by. Under the name of "Captain

Hardy," Thoreau celebrated this achievement of his townsman, upon which the hundreds who in summer stroll to the School of Philosophy in Mr. Alcott's orchard, now gaze with admiration,—bettered as it has been by the thirty years' toil and skill bestowed upon it since by Captain Moore's son and grandson. Thoreau said:

"Look across the fence into Captain Hardy's land. There 's a musician for you who knows how to make men dance for him in all weathers, — all sorts of men, — Paddies, felons, farmers, carpenters, painters, — yes, and trees, and grapes, and ice, and stone, — hot days, cold days. Beat that true Orpheus lyre if you can. He knows how to make men sow, dig, mow, and lay stone-wall; to make trees bear fruit God never gave them, and foreign grapes yield the juices of France and Spain, on his south side. He saves every drop of sap, as if it were his blood. See his cows, his horses, his swine! And he, the piper that plays the jig they all must dance, biped and quadruped, is the plainest, stupidest harlequin, in a coat of no colors. His are the woods, the waters, hills, and meadows. With one blast of his pipe he danced a thousand tons of gravel from yonder blowing sand-heap to the bog-meadow, where the English grass is waving over thirty acres; with another, he winded away sixty head of cattle in the spring, to the pastures of Peterboro' on the hills."

Such were and are the yeomen of Concord, among whom Thoreau spent his days, a friend to them and they to him, though each sometimes spoke churlishly of the other. He surveyed their wood-lots, laid out their roads, measured their fields and pastures for division among the heirs when a husbandman died, inspected their rivers and ponds, and exchanged information with them concerning the birds, the beasts, insects, flowers, crops, and trees. Their yearly Cattle Show in October was his chief festival, — one of the things he regretted, when living on the edge of New York Bay, and sighing for Fairhaven and White Pond. Without them the landscape of his native valley would not have been so dear to his eyes, and to their humble and perennial virtues he owed more inspiration than he would always confess.

He read in the crabbed Latin of those old Roman farmers, Cato, Varro, and musically-named Columella, and fancied the farmers of Concord were daily obeying

Cato's directions, who in turn was but repeating the maxims of a more remote antiquity.

"I see the old, pale-faced farmer walking beside his team, with contented thoughts," he says, "for the five thousandth time. This drama every day in the streets; this is the theatre I go to. . . . Human life may be transitory and full of trouble, but the perennial mind, whose survey extends from that spring to this, from Columella to Hosmer, is superior to change. I will identify myself with that which did not die with Columella, and will not die with Hosmer."

CHAPTER V.

THE TRANSCENDENTAL PERIOD.

ALTHOUGH Henry Thoreau would have been, in any place or time of the world's drama, a personage of note, it has already been observed, in regard to his career and his unique literary gift, that they were affected, and in some sort fashioned by the influences of the very time and place in which he found himself at the opening of life. It was the sunrise of New England Transcendentalism in which he first looked upon the spiritual world; when Carlyle in England, Alcott, Emerson, and Margaret Fuller in Massachusetts, were preparing their contemporaries in America for that modern Renaissance which has been so fruitful, for the last forty years, in high thought, vital religion, pure literature, and great deeds. And the place of his birth and breeding, the home of his affections, as it was the Troy, the Jerusalem, and the Rome of his imagination, was determined by Providence to be that very centre and shrine of Transcendentalism, the little village of Concord, which would have been saved from oblivion by his books, had it no other title to remembrance. Let it be my next effort, then, to give some hint — not a brief chronicle — of that extraordinary age, not yet ended (often as they tell us of its death and epitaph), now known to all men as the Transcendental Period. We must wait for after-times to fix its limits and determine its dawn and setting; but of its apparent beginning and course, one cycle coincided quite closely with the life of Thoreau. He was born in July, 1817, when Emerson was entering college at Cambridge, and Carlyle was wrestling "with doubt, fear, unbelief, mockery, and scoffing, in agony of spirit," at Edinburgh. He died in May, 1862, when the distinctly spiritual and literary era of Transcendentalism had closed, its years of preparation were over, and it had entered upon the conflict of political regeneration, for which Thoreau was constantly sounding the trumpet. In these forty-five years, — a longer period than the age of Pericles, or of the Medici, or of Queen Elizabeth, — New England Transcendentalism rose, climbed, and culminated, leaving results that, for our America, must be compared with those famous eras of civilization. Those ages, in fact, were well-nigh lost upon us, until Channing, Emerson, Thoreau, Margaret Fuller, and their fellowship, brought us into communication with the Greek, the Italian, and the noble Elizabethan revivals of genius and art. We had been living under the Puritan reaction, modified and politically fashioned by the more humane philosophy of the eighteenth century, while the freedom-breathing, but half-barbarizing influences of pioneer life in a new continent, had also turned aside the full force of English and Scotch Calvinism.

It is common to trace the so-called Transcendentalism of New England to Carlyle and Coleridge and Wordsworth in the mother-country, and to Goethe, Richter, and Kant in Germany; and there is a certain outward affiliation of this sort, which cannot be denied. But that which in our spiritual soil gave root to the foreign seeds thus wafted hitherward, was a certain inward tendency of high Calvinism and its counterpart, Quakerism, always welling forth in the American colonies. Now it inspired Cotton, Wheelwright, Sir Harry Vane, and Mistress Anne Hutchinson, in Massachusetts; now William Penn and his quaint brotherhood on the Delaware; now Jonathan Edwards and Sarah Pierpont, in Connecticut; and, again, John Woolman, the wandering Friend of God and man, in New Jersey, Nicholas Gilman, the convert of Whitefield, in New Hampshire, and Samuel Hopkins, the preacher of disinterested benevolence, in Rhode Island, held forth this noble doctrine of the Inner Light. It is a gospel peculiarly attractive to poets, so that even the loose-girt Davenant, who would fain think himself the left-hand son of Shakespeare, told gossiping old Aubrey that he believed the world, after a while, would settle into one religion, "an ingenious Quakerism,"—that is, a faith in divine communication that would yet leave some scope for men of wit like himself. How truly these American Calvinists and Quakers prefigured the mystical part of Concord philosophy, may be seen by a few of their sayings.

Jonathan Edwards, in 1723, when he was twenty years old, and the fair saint of his adoration was fifteen, thus wrote in his diary what he had seen and heard of Sarah Pierpont: —

"There is a young lady in New Haven who is beloved of that Great Being who made and rules the world; and there are certain seasons in which this Great Being, in some way or other invisible, comes to her and fills her mind with exceeding sweet delight, and she hardly cares for anything except to meditate on Him. Therefore, if you present all the world before her, with the richest of its treasures, she disregards it, and cares not for it, and is unmindful of any pain or affliction. She has a strange sweetness in her mind, and a singular purity in her affections; is most just and conscientious in all her conduct; and you could not persuade her to do anything wrong or sinful, if you would give her all the world, lest she should offend this Great Being. She will sometimes go about from place to place singing sweetly, and seems to be always full of joy and pleasure, and no one knows for what. She loves to be alone walking in the fields and groves, and seems to have some one invisible always conversing with her."

Nicholas Gilman, the parish minister of

little Durham, in New Hampshire,—being under concern of mind for his friend Whitefield, and the great man of New England, at that time, Sir William Pepperell, just setting forth for the capture of Louisburg —wrote to them in March, 1745,—to Sir William thus:—

"Do you indeed love the Lord? do you make the Lord your Guide and Counselor in ye affair? If you have a Soul, great as that Hero David of old, you will ask of the Lord, and not go till he bid you: David would not. If you are sincerely desirous to know and do your duty in that and every other respect, and seek of God in Faith, you shall know that, and everything else needful, one thing after another, as fast as you are prepared for it. But God will, doubtless, humble such as leave him out of their Schemes, as though his Providence was not at all concerned in the matter — whereas his Blessing is all in all."

To Whitefield, Gilman wrote in the same vein, on the same day:—

"Are you sufficiently sure that his call is from above, that he was moved by the Holy Ghost to this Expedition? Would it be no advantage to his Estate to win the place? May he not have a prospect of doubling his Wealth and Honours, if crowned with Success? What Demonstration has he given of being so entirely devoted to the Lord? He has a vast many Talents,—is it an easy thing for so Wise a man to become a Fool for Christ? so great a man to become a Little Child? so rich a man to crowd in at the Strait Gate of Conversion, and make so little noise? . . . If you see good to encourage the Expedition, be fully satisfy'd the project was formed in Heaven. Was the Lord first consulted in the affair? Did they wait for his Counsell?"

John Woolman, the New Jersey Quaker (born in 1720, died in 1772), said,—

"There is a principle which is pure, placed in the human mind, which, in different places and ages hath had different names; it is, however, pure, and proceeds from God. It is deep and inward, confined to no forms of religion, nor excluded from any, when the heart stands in perfect sincerity. In whomsoever this takes root and grows, they become brethren. That state in which every motion from the selfish spirit yieldeth to pure love, I may acknowlege with gratitude to the Father of Mercies, is often opened before me as a pearl to seek after."[1]

[1] The resemblance between some of John Woolman's utterances and those of Henry Thoreau has been noticed

That even the pious egotism and the laughable vagaries of Transcendentalism had their prototype in the private meditations of the New England Calvinists, is well known to such as have studied old diaries of the Massachusetts ministers. Thus, a minister of Malden (a successor of the awful Michael Wigglesworth, whose alleged poem, "The Day of Doom," as Cotton Mather thought, might perhaps "find our children till the Day itself arrives"), in his diary for 1735, thus enters his trying experiences with a "one-horse Shay," whose short life may claim comparison with that of the hundred-year master-piece of Dr. Holmes's deacon: —

"*January* 31. Bought a shay for £27 10*s*. The Lord grant it may be a comfort and blessing to my family.

by Whittier, who says of the New Jersey Quaker, "From his little farm on the Rancocas he looked out with a mingled feeling of wonder and sorrow upon the hurry and unrest of the world; he regarded the merely rich man with unfeigned pity. With nothing of his scorn, he had all of Thoreau's commiseration for people who went about, bowed down with the weight of broad acres and great houses on their backs." The "scorn" of Thoreau and the "pity" of Woolman, sprang from a common root, however.

"*March*, 1735. Had a safe and comfortable journey to York.

"*April* 24. Shay overturned, with my wife and I in it, yet neither of us much hurt. Blessed be our gracious Preserver! Part of the shay, as it lay upon one side, went over my wife, and yet she was scarcely anything hurt. How wonderful the preservation!

"*May* 5. Went to the Beach with three of the children. The Beast being frighted, when we were all out of the shay, overturned and broke it. I desire (I hope I desire it) that the Lord would teach me suitably to repent this Providence, to make suitable remarks on it, and to be suitably affected with it. Have I done well to get me a shay? Have I not been proud or too fond of this convenience? Do I exercise the faith in the divine care and protection which I ought to do? Should I not be more in my study, and less fond of diversion? Do I not withhold more than is meet from pious and charitable uses?

"*May* 15. Shay brought home; mending cost 30 shillings. Favored in this beyond expectation.

"*May* 16. My wife and I rode to Rumney Marsh. The Beast frighted several times."

At last this divine comedy ends with the pathetic conclusive line,—

"*June* 4. Disposed of my shay to the Rev. Mr. White."

I will not pause to dwell on the laughable episodes and queer characteristic features of the Transcendental Period, though such it had in abundance. They often served to correct the soberer absurdity with which our whole country was slipping unconsciously down the easy incline of national ruin and dishonor, — from which only a bloody civil war could at last save us. Thoreau saw this clearly, and his political utterances, paradoxical as they seemed in the two decades from 1840 to 1860, now read like the words of a prophet. But there are some points in the American Renaissance which may here be touched on, so much light do they throw on the times. It was a period of strange faiths and singular apocalypses — that of Charles Fourier being one. In February, 1843, Mr. Emerson, writing to Henry Thoreau from New York, where he was then lecturing, said: —

"Mr. Brisbane has just given me a faithful hour and a half of what he calls his principles, and he shames truer men by his fidelity and zeal; and already begins to hear the reverberations of his single voice from most of the States of the Union. He thinks himself sure of W. H. Channing here, as a good Fourierist. I laugh incredulous whilst he recites (for it seems always as if he was repeating paragraphs out of his master's book) descriptions of the self-augmenting potency of the solar system, which is destined to contain one hundred and thirty-two bodies, I believe, — and his urgent inculcation of our *stellar duties*. But it has its kernel of sound truth, and its insanity is so wide of the New York insanities that it is virtue and honor."

This was written a few months before Thoreau himself went to New York, and it was while there that he received from his friends in Concord and in Harvard, the wondrous account of Mr. Alcott's Paradise Regained at Fruitlands; where in due time Thoreau made his visit and inspected that Garden of Eden on the Coldspring Brook.

If Mr. Brisbane had his "stellar duties" and inculcated them in others, the Brook Farmers of 1842–43 had their planetary mission also; namely, to cultivate the face of the planet they inhabited, and to do it with their own hands, as Adam and Noah did. Of the Brook Farm enterprise much has been written, and much more will be; but concerning the more individual dream of Thoreau's friends at "Fruitlands," less is known; and I may quote a few pages concerning it from Thoreau's correspondence. While Thoreau was at Staten Island in 1843, Mr. Emerson wrote to him often, giving the news of Concord as a Transcendental capital. In May of that year we have this intelligence: —

"Ellery Channing is well settled in his house, and works very steadily thus far, and our intercourse is very agreeable to me. Young Ball (B. W.) has been to see me, and is a prodigious reader and a youth of great promise, — born, too, in the good town. Mr. Hawthorne is well, and Mr. Alcott and Mr. Lane are revolving a purchase in Harvard of ninety acres."

This was "Fruitlands," described in the "Dial" for 1843, and which Charles Lane himself describes in a letter soon to be cited. In June, 1843, Mr. Emerson again sends tidings from Concord, where the Fitchburg railroad was then building: —

"The town is full of Irish, and the woods of engineers, with theodolite and red flag, singing out their feet and inches to each other from station to station. Near Mr. Alcott's (the Hosmer cottage) the road is already begun. From Mr. A. and Mr. Lane at Harvard we have yet heard nothing. They went away in good spirits, having sent 'Wood Abram' and Larned, and William Lane before them with horse and plow, a few days in advance, to begin the spring work. Mr. Lane paid me a long visit, in which he was more than I had ever known him gentle and open; and it was impossible not to sympathize with and honor projects that so often seem without feet or hands. They have near a hundred acres of land which they do not want, and no house, which they want first of all. But they account this an advantage, as it gives them the occasion they so much desire, — of building after their own idea. In the event of their attracting to their company a carpenter or two, which is not impossible, it would be a great pleasure to see their building, — which could hardly fail to be new and beautiful. They have fifteen acres of woodland, with good timber."

Then, passing in a moment from "Fruitlands" to Concord woods, Thoreau's friend writes: —

"Ellery Channing is excellent company, and we walk in all directions. He remembers you with great faith and hope, thinks you ought not to see Concord again these ten years; that you ought to grind up fifty Concords in your mill; and much other opinion and counsel he holds in store on this topic. Hawthorne walked with me yesterday afternoon, and not until after our return did I read his 'Celestial Railroad,' which has a serene strength we cannot afford not to praise, in this low life. I have letters from Miss Fuller at Niagara. She found it sadly cold and rainy at the Falls."

Not so with Mr. Alcott and Mr. Lane in the first flush of their hopes at Fruitlands. On the 9th of June, — the date of the letter just quoted being June 7, — Mr. Lane writes to Thoreau: —

"DEAR FRIEND, — The receipt of two acceptable numbers of the 'Pathfinder' reminds me that I am not altogether forgotten by one who, if not in the busy world, is at least much nearer to it externally than I am. Busy indeed we all are, since our removal here; but so recluse is our position, that with the world at large we have scarcely any connection. You may possibly have heard that, after all our efforts during the spring had failed to place us in connection with the earth, and Mr. Alcott's journey to Oriskany and Vermont had turned out a blank, — one afternoon in the latter part of May, Providence sent to us the legal owner of a slice of the planet in this township (Harvard), with whom we have been enabled to conclude for the concession of his rights. It is very remotely placed, nearly three miles beyond the village, without a road, surrounded by a beautiful green landscape of fields and woods, with the distance filled up by some of the loftiest mountains in the State. The views are, indeed, most poetic and inspiring. You have no doubt seen the neighborhood; but from these very fields, where you may at once be at home and out, there is enough to love and revel in for sympathetic souls like yours. On the estate are about fourteen acres of wood, part of it extremely pleasant as a retreat, a very sylvan realization, which only wants a Thoreau's mind to elevate it to classic beauty.

"I have some imagination that you are not so happy and so well housed in your present position as you would be here amongst us; although at present there is much hard manual labor, — so much that, as you perceive, my usual handwriting is very greatly suspended. We have only two associates in addition to our own families; our house accommodations are poor and scanty; but the greatest want is of good female aid. Far too much labor devolves on Mrs. Alcott. If you should light on any such assistance, it would be charitable to give it a direction this way. We may, perhaps, be rather particular about the quality; but the conditions will pretty well determine the acceptability of the parties without a direct adjudication on our part. For though to me our mode of life is luxurious in the highest degree, yet generally it seems to be thought that the setting aside of all impure diet, dirty habits, idle thoughts, and selfish feelings, is a course of self-denial, scarcely to be encountered or even thought of in such an alluring world as this in which we dwell.

"Besides the busy occupations of each succeeding day, we form, in this ample theatre of hope, many forthcoming scenes. The nearer little copse is designed as the site of the cottages. Fountains can be made to descend from their granite sources on the hill-slope to every apartment if required. Gardens are to displace the warm grazing glades on the south, and numerous human beings, instead of cattle, shall here enjoy existence. The farther wood offers to the naturalist and the poet an exhaustless haunt; and a short cleaning of the brook would connect our boat with the Nashua. Such are the designs which Mr. Alcott and I have just sketched, as, resting from planting, we walked round this reserve.

"In your intercourse with the dwellers in the great city, have you alighted on Mr. Edward Palmer, who studies with Dr. Beach, the Herbalist? He will, I think, from his previous nature-love, and his affirmations to Mr. Alcott, be animated on learning of this actual wooing and winning of Nature's regards. We should be most happy to see him with us. Having become so far actual, from the real, we might fairly enter into the typical, if he could help us in any way to types of the true metal. We have not passed away from home, to see or hear of the world's doings, but the report has reached us of Mr. W. H. Channing's fellowship with the Phalansterians, and of his eloquent speeches in their behalf. Their progress will be much aided by his accession. To both these worthy men be pleased to suggest our humanest sentiments. While they stand amongst men, it is well to find them acting out the truest possible at the moment.

"Just before we heard of this place, Mr. Alcott had projected a settlement at the Cliffs on the Concord River, cutting down wood and building a cottage; but so many more facilities were presented here that we quitted the old classic town for one which is to be not less renowned. As far as I could judge, our absence promised little pleasure to our old Concord friends; but at signs of progress I presume they rejoiced with, dear friend, Yours faithfully,

"CHARLES LANE."

Another Palmer than the Edward here mentioned became an inmate of "Fruitlands," and, in course of time its owner; the abandoned paradise, which was held by Mr. Lane and Mr. Alcott for less than a year, is now the property of his son. Mr. Lane, after a time, returned to England and died there; Mr. Alcott to Concord, where, in 1845, he aided Thoreau in building his hut by Walden. Mr. Channing (the nephew and biographer of Dr. Channing) continued his connection with the "Phalansterians" in New Jersey until 1849 or later, for in that year Fredrika Bremer found him dwelling and preaching among them, at the "North American Phalanstery," to which he had been invited from his Unitarian parish in Cincinnati, about the time that Brook Farm was made a community, and before Mr. Alcott's dream had taken earthly shape at "Fruitlands." The account given by Miss Bremer of the terms upon which Mr. Channing was thus invited to New Jersey, show what was the spirit of Transcendentalism then, on its social side. They said to him, —

"Come to us, — be our friend and spiritual shepherd, but in perfect freedom. Follow your own inspiration, — preach, talk to us, how and when it appears best to you. We undertake to provide for your pecuniary wants; live free from anxiety, how, and where you will; but teach us how we should live and work; our homes and our hearts are open to you."

It was upon such terms as this, honorable alike to those who gave and those who received, that much of the intellectual and spiritual work of the Transcendental revival was done. There was another and an unsocial side to the movement also, which Mr. Emerson early described in these words, that apply to Thoreau and to Alcott at one period: —

"It is a sign of our times, conspicuous to the coarsest observer, that many intelligent and religious persons withdraw themselves from the common labors and competitions of the market and the caucus, and betake themselves to a solitary and critical way of living, from which no solid fruit has yet appeared to justify their separation. They hold themselves aloof; they feel the disproportion between themselves and the work offered them, and they prefer to ramble in the country and perish of ennui, to the degradation of such charities and such ambitions as the city can propose to them. They are striking work and crying out for somewhat worthy to do.

They are lonely; the spirit of their writing and conversation is lonely; they repel influences; they shun general society; they incline to shut themselves in their chamber in the house; to live in the country rather than in the town; and to find their tasks and amusements in solitude. They are not good citizens, not good members of society; unwillingly they bear their part of the public and private burdens; they do not willingly share in the public charities, in the public religious rites, in the enterprise of education, of missions, foreign or domestic, in the abolition of the slave trade, or in the temperance society. They do not even like to vote. The philanthropists inquire whether Transcendentalism does not mean sloth; they had as lief hear that their friend is dead, as that he is a Transcendentalist; for then is he paralyzed, and can do nothing for humanity."

It was this phase of Transcendentalism that gave most anxiety to Thoreau's good old pastor, Dr. Ripley, who early foresaw what immediate fruit might be expected from this fair tree of mysticism, — this "burning bush" which had started up, all at once, in the very garden of his parsonage. I know few epistles more pathetic in their humility and concern for the future, than one which Dr. Ripley addressed to Dr. Channing in February, 1839, after hearing and meditating on the utterances of Alcott, Emerson, Thoreau, George Ripley, and the other "apostles of the newness," who disturbed with their oracles the quiet air of his parish. He wrote: —

"Denied, as I am, the privilege of going from home, of visiting and conversing with enlightened friends, and of reading even; broken down with the infirmities of age, and subject to fits that deprive me of reason and the use of my limbs, I feel it a duty to be patient and submissive to the will of God, who is too wise to err, and too good to injure. Some reason is left, — my mental powers, though weak, are yet awake, and I long to be doing something for good. The contrast between paper and ink is so strong, that I can write better than do anything else. In this way I take the liberty to express to you a few thoughts, which you will receive as well-meant and sincere. . . .

"We may certainly assume that whatever is unreasonable, self-contradictory, and destitute of common sense, is erroneous. Should we not be likely to find the truth, in all moral subjects, were we to make more use of plain reason and common sense? I know that our modern spec ulators, Transcendentalists, or, as they prefer to be called, Realists, presume to follow Reason in her purest dictates. her sublime and unfrequented regions. They presume, by her power, not only to discover what is truth, but to judge of revealed truth. But is not their whole process marred by leaving out common sense, by which mankind are generally governed? That superiority which places a man above the power of doing good to his fellow-men seems to me not very desirable. I honor most the man who transcends others in capacity and disposition to do good, and whose daily practice corresponds with his profession. Here I speak of professed Christians. I would not treat with disrespect and severe censure men who advance sentiments which I may neither approve nor understand, provided their authors be men of learning, piety, and holy lives. The speculations and novel opinions of *such* men rarely prove injurious. Nevertheless, I would that their mental endowments might find a better method of doing good, — a more simple and intelligible manner of informing and reforming their fellow-men. . . .

"The hope of the gospel is my hope, my consolation, support and rejoicing. Such is my state of health that death is constantly before me; no minute would it be unexpected. I am waiting in faith and hope, but humble and penitent for my imperfections and faults. The prayer of the publican, 'God be merciful to me a sinner!' is never forgotten. I have hoped to see and converse with you, but now despair. If you shall think I use too much freedom with you, charge it to the respect and esteem which are cherished for your character by your affectionate friend and brother, E. RIPLEY.

"CONCORD, *February* 26, 1839."

At this time Dr. Ripley was almost eighty-eight, and he lived two years longer, to mourn yet more pathetically over the change of times and manners. "It was fit," said Emerson, "that in the fall of laws, this loyal man should die." But the young men who succeeded him were no less loyal to the unwritten laws, and from their philosophy, which to the old theologian seemed so misty and unreal, there flowered forth, in due season, the most active and world-wide philanthropies. Twenty years after this pastoral epistle, there came to Concord another Christian of the antique type, more Puritan and Hebraic than Dr. Ripley himself, yet a Transcendentalist, too, — and JOHN BROWN found no lack of practical good-will in Thoreau, Alcott,

Emerson, and the other Transcendentalists. The years had "come full circle," the Sibyl had burnt her last prophetic book, and the new æon was about to open with the downfall of slavery

CHAPTER VI

EARLY ESSAYS IN AUTHORSHIP.

It has been a common delusion, not yet quite faded away, that the chief Transcendentalists were but echoes of each other, — that Emerson imitated Carlyle, Thoreau and Alcott imitated Emerson, and so on to the end of the chapter. No doubt that the atmosphere of each of these men affected the others, nor that they shared a common impulse communicated by what Matthew Arnold likes to call the *Zeitgeist*, — the ever-felt spirit of the time. In the most admirable of the group, who is called by preëminence "the Sage of Concord," — the poet Emerson, — there has been an outbreathing inspiration as profound as that of the *Zeitgeist* himself; so that even Hawthorne, the least susceptible of men, found himself affected as he says, "after living for three years within the subtle influence of an intellect like Emerson's." But, in fact, Thoreau brought to his intellectual tasks an originality as marked as Emerson's, if not so brilliant and star-like — a patience far greater than his, and a proud independence that makes him the most solitary of modern thinkers. I have been struck by these qualities in reading his yet unknown first essays in authorship, the juvenile papers he wrote while in college, from the age of seventeen to that of twenty, before Emerson had published anything except his first little volume, "Nature," and while Thoreau, like other young men, was reading Johnson and Goldsmith, Addison and the earlier English classics, from Milton backward to Chaucer. Let me therefore quote from these papers, carefully preserved by him, with their dates, and sometimes with the marks of the rhetorical professor on their margins. Along with these may be cited some of his earlier verses, in which a sentiment more purely human and almost amatory appears, than in the later and colder, if higher flights of his song.

The earliest writings of Thoreau, placed in my hands by his literary executor, Mr.

Harrison Blake of Worcester, are the first of his Cambridge essays, technically called "themes" and "forensics." These began several years before his daily journals were kept, namely, in 1834; and it is curious that one of them, dated January 17, 1835, but written in 1834, recommends "keeping a private journal or record of our thoughts, feelings, studies, and daily experience." This is precisely what Thoreau did from 1837 till his death; and it may be interesting to see what reasons the boy of seventeen advanced for the practice. He says:—

"As those pieces which the painter sketches for his own amusement, in his leisure hours, are often superior to his most elaborate productions, so it is that ideas often suggest themselves to us spontaneously, as it were, far surpassing in beauty those which arise in the mind upon applying ourselves to any particular subject. Hence, could a machine be invented which would instantaneously arrange upon paper each idea as it occurs to us, without any exertion on our part, how extremely useful would it be considered! The relation between this and the practice of keeping a journal is obvious. . . . If each one would employ a certain portion of each day in looking back upon the time which has passed, and in writing down his thoughts and feelings, in reckoning up his daily gains, that he may be able to detect whatever false coins may have crept into his coffers, and, as it were, in settling accounts with his mind, — not only would his daily experience be greatly increased, since his feelings and ideas would thus be more clearly defined, — but he would be ready to turn over a new leaf (having carefully perused the preceding one) and would not continue to glance carelessly over the same page, without being able to distinguish it from a new one."

This is ingenious, quaint, and mercantile, bespeaking the hereditary bent of his family to trade and orderly accounts; but what follows in the same essay is more to the purpose, as striking the key-note of Thoreau's whole after-life. He adds: —

"Most of us are apt to neglect the study of our own characters, thoughts, and feelings, and, for the purpose of forming our own minds, look to others, *who should merely be considered as different editions of the same great work.* To be sure, it would be well for us to examine the various copies, that we might detect any errors; yet it would be foolish for one *to borrow a work which he possessed himself, but had not perused.*"

The earliest record of the day's observations which I find is dated a few months later than this (April 20, 1835), when Henry Thoreau was not quite eighteen, and relates to the beauties of nature. The first passage describes a Sunday prospect from the garret window of his father's house, (afterwards the residence of Mr. William Munroe, the benefactor of the Concord Library), on the main street of the village. He writes: —

"'T was always my delight to monopolize the little Gothic window which overlooked the kitchen-garden, particularly of a Sabbath afternoon; when all around was quiet, and Nature herself was taking her afternoon nap, — when the last peal of the bell in the neighboring steeple,

'Swinging slow with sullen roar,'

had 'left the vale to *solitude* and *me*,' and the very air scarcely dared breathe, lest it should disturb the universal calm. Then did I use, with eyes upturned, to gaze upon the clouds, and, allowing my imagination to wander, search for flaws in their rich drapery, that I might get a peep at that world beyond, which they seem intended to veil from our view. Now is my attention engaged by a truant hawk, as, like a messenger from those ethereal regions, he issues from the bosom of a cloud, and, at first a mere speck in the distance, comes circling onward, exploring every seeming creek, and rounding every jutting precipice. And now, his mission ended, what can be more majestic than his stately flight, as he wheels around some towering pine, enveloped in a cloud of smaller birds that have united to expel him from their premises."

The second passage, under the same date, seems to describe earlier and repeated visits, made by his elder brother John and himself, to a hill which was always a favorite resort of Thoreau's, Fairhaven Cliffs, overlooking the river-bay, known as "Fairhaven," a mile or two up the river from Concord village toward Sudbury: —

"In the freshness of the dawn my brother and I were ever ready to enjoy a stroll to a certain cliff, distant a mile or more, where we were wont to climb to the highest peak, and seating ourselves on some rocky platform, catch the first ray of the morning sun, as it gleamed upon the smooth, still river, wandering in sullen silence far below. The approach to the precipice is by no means calculated to prepare one for the glorious *dénouement* at hand. After following for some time a delightful path that winds through the woods, occasionally crossing a rippling brook, and not forgetting to visit a sylvan dell, whose solitude is made audible by the unwearied tinkling of a crystal spring, — you suddenly emerge from the trees upon a flat and mossy rock, which forms the summit of a beetling crag. The feelings which come over one on first beholding this freak of nature are indescribable. The giddy height, the iron-bound rock, the boundless horizon open around, and the beautiful river at your feet, with its green and sloping banks, fringed with trees and shrubs of every description, are calculated to excite in the beholder emotions of no common occurrence, — to inspire him with noble and sublime emotions. The eye wanders over the broad and seemingly compact surface of the slumbering forest on the opposite side of the stream, and catches an occasional glimpse of a little farm-house, 'resting in a green hollow, and lapped in the bosom of plenty;' while a gentle swell of the river, a rustic, and fortunately rather old-looking bridge on the right, with the cloud-like Wachusett in the distance, give a finish and beauty to the landscape, that is rarely to be met with even in our own fair land. This interesting spot, if we may believe tradition, was the favorite haunt of the red man, before the axe of his pale-faced visitor had laid low its loftier honors, or his 'strong water' had wasted the energies of the race."

Here we have a touch of fine writing, natural in a boy who had read Irving and Goldsmith, and exaggerating a little the dimensions of the rocks and rills of which he wrote. But how smooth the flow of description, how well-placed the words, how sure and keen the eye of the young observer! To this mount of vision did Thoreau and his friends constantly resort in after years, and it was on the plateau beneath that Mr. Alcott, in 1843, was about to cut down the woods and build his Paradise, when a more inviting fate, as he thought, beckoned his English friend Lane and himself to "Fruitlands," in the distant town of Harvard. At some time after this, perhaps while Thoreau was encamped at Walden with his books and his flute, Mr. Emerson sent him the following note, which gives us now a glimpse into that Arcadia: —

"Will you not come up to the Cliff this P. M., at any hour convenient to you, where our ladies will be greatly gratified to see you? and the more, they say, if you will bring your flute for the echo's sake, though now the wind blows.

"R. W. E.

"Monday, 1 o'clock P. M."

It does not appear that Thoreau wrote verses at this time, though he was a great reader of the best poetry, — of Milton very early, and with constant admiration and quotation. Thus, in a college essay of 1835, on "Simplicity of Style," he has this passage concerning the Bible and Milton: —

"The most sublime and noblest precepts may be conveyed in a plain and simple strain. The Scriptures afford abundant proof of this. What images can be more natural, what sentiments of greater weight and at the same time more noble and exalted than those with which they abound? They possess no local or relative ornament which may be lost in a translation; clothed in whatever dress, they still retain their peculiar beauties. Here is simplicity itself. Every one allows this, every one admires it, yet how few attain to it! The union of wisdom and simplicity is plainly hinted at in the following lines of Milton: —

'Suspicion sleeps
At Wisdom's gate, and to *Simplicity*
Resigns her charge.'"

Early in 1837 Thoreau wrote an elaborate paper, though of no great length, on Milton's "L'Allegro" and "Il Penseroso," with many quotations, in course of which he said: —

"These poems place Milton in an entirely new and extremely pleasing light to the reader, who was previously familiar with him as the author of 'Paradise Lost' alone. If before he venerated, he may now admire and love him. The immortal Milton seems for a space to have put on mortality, — to have snatched a moment from the weightier cares of Heaven and Hell, to wander for a while among the sons of men. . . . I have dwelt upon the poet's beauties and not so much as glanced at his blemishes. A pleasing image, or a fine sentiment loses none of its charms, though Burton, or Beaumont and Fletcher, or Marlowe, or Sir Walter Raleigh, may have written something very similar, — or even in another connection, may have used the identical word, whose aptness we so much admire. That always appeared to me a contemptible kind of criticism which, deliberately and in cold blood, can dissect the sublimest passage, and take pleasure in the detection of slight verbal incongruities; when applied to Milton, it is little better than sacrilege."

The moral view taken by the young collegian in these essays is quite as interesting as the literary opinions, or the ease of his style. In September, 1835, discussing punishments, he says: —

"Certainty is more effectual than severity of punishment. No man will deliberately cut his own fingers. Some have asked, 'Cannot reward be substituted for punishment? Is hope a less powerful incentive to action than fear? When a political pharmacopœia has the command of both ingredients, wherefore employ the bitter instead of the sweet?' This reasoning is absurd. Does a man deserve to be rewarded for refraining from murder? Is the greatest virtue merely negative? or does it rather consist in the performance of a thousand every-day duties, hidden from the eye of the world?"

In an essay on the effect of story-telling, written in 1836, he says: —

"The story of the world never ceases to interest. The child enchanted by the melodies of Mother Goose, the scholar pondering 'the tale of Troy divine,' and the historian breathing the atmosphere of past ages, — all manifest the same passion, are alike the creatures of curiosity. The same passion for the novel (somewhat modified, to be sure), that is manifested in our early days, leads us, in after-life, when the sprightliness and credulity of youth have given way to the reserve and skepticism of manhood, to the more serious, though scarcely less wonderful annals of the world. The love of stories and of story-telling cherishes a purity of heart, a frankness and candor of disposition, a respect for what is generous and elevated, a contempt for what is mean and dishonorable, and tends to multiply merry companions and never-failing friends."

In March, 1837, in an essay on the source of our feeling of the sublime, Thoreau says:—

"The emotion excited by the sublime is the most unearthly and god-like we mortals experience. It depends for the peculiar strength with which it takes hold on and occupies the mind, upon a principle which lies at the foundation of that worship which we pay to the Creator himself. And is fear the foundation of that worship? Is fear the ruling principle of our religion? Is it not rather the mother of superstition? Yes, that principle which prompts us to pay an involuntary homage to the infinite, the incomprehensible, the sublime, forms the very basis of our religion. It is a principle implanted in us by our Maker, a part of our very selves; we cannot eradicate it, we cannot resist it; fear may be overcome, death may be despised; but the infinite, the sublime seize upon the soul and disarm it. We may overlook them, or rather fall short of them; we may pass them by, but, so sure as we meet them face to face, we yield."

Speaking of national characteristics, he says: —

"It is not a little curious to observe how man, the boasted lord of creation, is the slave of a name, a mere sound. How much mischief have those magical words, North, South, East, and West caused! Could we rest satisfied with one mighty, all-embracing West, leaving the other three cardinal points to the Old World, methinks we should not have cause for so much apprehension about the preservation of the Union."

(This was written in February, 1837.) Before he had reached the age of nineteen he thus declared his independence of foreign opinion, while asserting its general sway over American literature, in 1836: —

"We are, as it were, but colonies. True, we have declared our independence, and gained our liberty, but we have dissolved only the political bands which connected us with Great Britain; though we have rejected her tea, she still supplies us with food for the mind. The aspirant to fame must breathe the atmosphere of foreign parts, and learn to talk about things which the homebred student never dreamed of, if he would have his talents appreciated or his opinion regarded by his countrymen. Ours are authors of the day, they bid fair to outlive their works; they are too fashionable to write for posterity. True, there are some amongst us, who can contemplate the babbling brook, without, in imagination, polluting its waters with a mill-wheel; but even they are prone to sing of skylarks and nightingales perched on hedges, to the neglect of the homely robin-redbreast and the straggling rail-fences of their own native land."

So early did he take this position, from which he never varied.

In May, 1837, we find another note of his opening life, in an essay on Paley's "Common Reasons." He says: —

"Man does not wantonly rend the meanest tie that binds him to his fellows; he would not stand aloof, even in his prejudices, did not the stern demands of truth require it. He is ready enough to float with the tide, and when he does stem the current of popular opinion, sincerity, at least, must nerve his arm. He has not only the burden of proof, but that of reproof to support. We may call him a fanatic, an enthusiast; but these are titles of honor; they signify the devotion and entire surrendering of himself to his cause. So far as my experience goes, man *never* seriously maintained an objectionable principle, doctrine, or theory; error *never* had a sincere defender; her disciples were *never* enthusiasts. This is strong language, I confess, but I do not rashly make use of it. We are told that 'to err is human,' but I would rather call it inhuman, if I may use the word in this sense. I speak not of those errors that have to do with facts and occurrences, but rather, errors of judgment."

Here we have that bold generalization and that calm love of paradox which mark his later style. The lofty imagination was always his, too, as where this youth of nineteen says in the same essay: —

"Mystery is yet afar off, — it is but a cloud in the distance, whose shadow, as it flits across the landscape, gives a pleasing variety to the scene. But as the perfect day approaches, its morning light discovers the dark and straggling clouds, which at first skirted the horizon, assembling as at a signal, and as they expand and multiply, rolling slowly onward to the zenith, till, at last, the whole heavens, if we except a faint glimmering in the East, are overshadowed."

What a confident and flowing movement of thought is here! like the prose of Milton or Jeremy Taylor, but with a more restrained energy.

"Duty," writes the young moralist in another

essay of 1837, "is one and invariable; it requires no impossibilities, nor can it ever be disregarded with impunity; so far as it exists, it is binding; and, if all duties are binding, so as on no account to be neglected, how can one bind stronger than another?" "None but the highest minds can attain to moral excellence. With by far the greater part of mankind religion is a habit; or rather habit is religion. However paradoxical it may seem, it appears to me that to reject *religion* is the first step towards moral excellence; at least no man ever attained to the highest degree of the latter by any other road. Could infidels live double the number of years allotted to other mortals, they would become patterns of excellence. So, too, of all true poets, —they would neglect the beautiful for the true."

I suspect that Thoreau's first poems date from the year 1837–38, since the "big red journal," in which they were copied, was begun in October, 1837. The verses entitled, "To the Maiden in the East," were, I imagine, among the first, though this is not certain; and near these in time was that poem called "Sympathy," which was the first of his writings to appear in Mr. Emerson's "Dial." These were both addressed, we are told, to the same maiden, with whom, the legend says, both Henry and John Thoreau were in love. Neither of these poems shows any imitation of Mr. Emerson, whose own verses at that time were mostly unpublished, though he sometimes read them in private to his friends. But like most of Thoreau's verses, these indicate a close familiarity with the Elizabethan literature, and what directly followed it, in the time of the Stuarts. The measure of "Sympathy" was that of Davenant's "Gondibert," which Thoreau, almost alone of his contemporaries, had read; the thought was above Davenant, and ranged with Raleigh and Spenser. These verses will not soon be forgotten: —

"Lately, alas! I knew a gentle boy,
  Whose features all were cast in Virtue's mould,
As one she had designed for Beauty's toy,
  But after manned him for her own stronghold.

"Say not that Cæsar was victorious,
  With toil and strife who stormed the House of Fame;
In other sense this youth was glorious,
  Himself a kingdom wheresoe'er he came.

. . . .

"Eternity may not the chance repeat,
  But I must tread my single way alone,

In sad remembrance that we once did meet,
  And know that bliss irrevocably gone.

"The spheres henceforth my elegy shall sing,
  For elegy has other subject none;
Each strain of music in my ears shall ring
  Knell of departure from that other one.

. . . .

"Is 't then too late the damage to repair?
  Distance, forsooth, from my weak grasp hath reft
The empty husk, and clutched the useless tare,
  But in my hands the wheat and kernel left.

"If I but love that virtue which he is,
  Though it be scented in the morning air,
Still shall we be dearest acquaintances,
  Nor mortals know a sympathy more rare."

The other poem seems to have been written earlier, before the separation of which this so loftily speaks; and it vibrates with a tenderer chord than sympathy. It begins, —

"Low in the eastern sky
Is set thy glancing eye,"

and then it goes on with the picture of lover-like things, — the thrushes and the flowers, until, he says,

"The trees a welcome waved,
And lakes their margin laved,
When thy free mind
To my retreat did wind."

Then comes the Persian dialect of high love: —

"It was a summer eve, —
The air did gently heave,
While yet a low-hung cloud
Thy eastern skies did shroud;
The lightning's silent gleam
Startling my drowsy dream,
Seemed like the flash
Under thy dark eyelash.

. . . .

"I 'll be thy Mercury,
Thou, Cytherea to me, —
Distinguished by thy face
The earth shall learn my place.
As near beneath thy light
Will I outwear the night,
With mingled ray
Leading the westward way."

"Let us," said Hafiz, "break up the tiresome roof of heaven into new forms," — and with as bold a flight did this young poet pass to his "stellar duties." Then dropping to the Concord meadow again, like the tuneful lark, he chose a less celestial path

"Of gentle slope and wide,
As thou wert by my side;
I 'll walk with gentle pace,
And choose the smoothest place,

And careful dip the oar,
And shun the winding shore,
And gently steer my boat
Where water-lilies float,
And cardinal flowers
Stand in their sylvan bowers."

A frivolous question has sometimes been raised whether the young Thoreau knew what love was, like the Sicilian shepherd, who found him a native of the rocks, a lion's whelp. With his poet-nature, he early gathered this experience, and passed on; praising afterwards the lion's nature in the universal god: —

"Implacable is Love, —
Foes may be bought or teased
From their hostile intent, —
But he goes unappeased
Who is on kindness bent.

"There 's nothing in the world, I know,
That can escape from Love,
For every depth it goes below,
And every height above."

The Red Journal of five hundred and ninety-six long pages, in which the early verses occur, was the first collection of Thoreau's systematic diarizing. It ran on from October, 1837, to June, 1840, and was succeeded by another journal of three hundred and ninety-six pages, which was finished early in 1841. He wrote his first lecture (on Society) in March, 1838, and read it before the Concord Lyceum in the Freemasons' Hall, April 11, 1838. In the December following he wrote a memorable essay on "Sound and Silence," and in February, 1840, wrote his "first printed paper of consequence," as he says, on "Aulus Perseus Flaccus." The best of the early verses seem to have been written in 1837–41. His contributions to the "Dial," which he helped edit, were taken from his journals, and ran through nearly every number from July, 1840, to April, 1844, when that magazine ceased.

For these papers he received nothing but the thanks of Emerson and the praise of a few readers. Miss Elizabeth Peabody, in February, 1843, wrote to Thoreau, that "the regular income of the 'Dial' does not pay the cost of its printing and paper; yet there are readers enough to support it, if they would only subscribe; and they will subscribe, if they are convinced that only by doing so can they secure its continuance." They did not subscribe, and in the spring of 1844 it came to an end.

In 1842 Thoreau took a walk to Wachusett, his nearest mountain, and the journal of this excursion was printed in the "Boston Miscellany" of 1843. In it occurred the verses, written at least as early as 1841, in which he addresses the mountains of his horizon, Monadnoc, Wachusett, and the Peterborough Hills of New Hampshire. These verses were for some time in the hands of Margaret Fuller, for publication in the "Dial," if she saw fit, but she returned them with the following characteristic letter, — the first addressed by her to Thoreau: —

"[CONCORD] 18*th October*, 1841.

"I do not find the poem on the mountains improved by mere compression, though it might be by fusion and glow. Its merits to me are, a noble recognition of Nature, two or three manly thoughts, and, in one place, a plaintive music. The image of the ships does not please me originally. It illustrates the greater by the less, and affects me as when Byron compares the light on Jura to that of the dark eye of woman. I cannot define my position here, and a large class of readers would differ from me. As the poet goes on to —

"Unhewn primeval timber,
For knees so stiff, for masts so limber."

he seems to chase an image, already rather forced, into conceits.

"Yet, now that I have some knowledge of the man, it seems there is no objection I could make to his lines (with the exception of such offenses against taste as the lines about the humors of the eye, as to which we are already agreed), which I would not make to himself. He is healthful, rare, of open eye, ready hand, and noble scope. He sets no limits to his life, nor to the invasions of nature; he is not willfully pragmatical, cautious, ascetic, or fantastical. But he is as yet a somewhat bare hill, which the warm gales of Spring have not visited. Thought lies too detached, truth is seen too much in detail; we can number and mark the substances imbedded in the rock. Thus his verses are startling as much as stern; the thought does not excuse its conscious existence by letting us see its relation with life; there is a want of fluent music. Yet what could a companion do at present, unless to tame the guardian of the Alps too early? Leave him at peace amid his native snows. He is friendly; he will find the generous office that shall educate him. It is not a soil for the citron and the rose, but for the whortleberry, the pine, or the heather.

"The unfolding of affections, a wider and

deeper human experience, the harmonizing influences of other natures, will mould the man and melt his verse. He will seek thought less and find knowledge the more. I can have no advice or criticism for a person so sincere; but, if I give my impression of him, I will say, 'He says too constantly of Nature, she is mine.' She is not yours till you have been more hers. Seek the lotus, and take a draught of rapture. Say not so confidently, all places, all occasions are alike. This will never come true till you have found it false.

"I do not know that I have more to say now; perhaps these words will say nothing to you. If intercourse should continue, perhaps a bridge may be made between two minds so widely apart; for I apprehended you in spirit, and you did not seem to mistake me so widely as most of your kind do. If you should find yourself inclined to write to me, as you thought you might, I dare say, many thoughts would be suggested to me; many have already, by seeing you from day to day. Will you finish the poem in your own way, and send it for the 'Dial'? Leave out

"And seem to milk the sky."

The image is too low; Mr. Emerson thought so too.

"Farewell! May truth be irradiated by

Beauty! Let me know whether you go to the lonely hut,[1] and write to me about Shakespeare, if you read him there. I have many thoughts about him, which I have never yet been led to express.

MARGARET F.

"The penciled paper Mr. E. put into my hands. I have taken the liberty to copy it. You expressed one day my own opinion, — that the moment such a crisis is passed, we may speak of it. There is no need of artificial delicacy, of secrecy; it keeps its own secrets; it cannot be made false. Thus you will not be sorry that I have seen the paper. Will you not send me some other records of the *good week?*"

"Faithful are the wounds of a friend." This searching criticism would not offend Thoreau; nor yet the plainness with which the same tongue told the faults of a prose paper — perhaps "The Recruit," — which Margaret rejected in this note: —

"[CONCORD] 1st *December* (1841).

"I am to blame for so long detaining your manuscript. But my thoughts have been so engaged that I have not found a suitable hour to re-read it as I wished, till last night. This second reading only confirms my impression from the

[1] The Hollowell Place, no doubt.

first. The essay is rich in thoughts, and I should be *pained* not to meet it again. But then, the thoughts seem to me so out of their natural order, that I cannot read it through without *pain*. I never once feel myself in a stream of thought, but seem to hear the grating of tools on the mosaic. It is true, as Mr. Emerson says, that essays not to be compared with this have found their way into the 'Dial.' But then, these are more unassuming in their tone, and have an air of quiet good-breeding, which induces us to permit their presence. Yours is so rugged that it ought to be commanding."

These were the years of Thoreau's apprenticeship in literature, and many were the tasks and mortifications he must endure before he became a master of the writer's art.

CHAPTER VII.

FRIENDS AND COMPANIONS.

"MARGARET FULLER," says William Henry Channing, "was indeed The Friend; this was her vocation." It was no less the vocation of Thoreau, though in a more lofty, unvarying, and serene manner.

"Literally," says the friend who best knew him, "his views of friendship were high and noble. Those who loved him never had the least reason to regret it. He made no useless professions, never asked one of those questions that destroy all relation; but he was on the spot at the time, and had so much of human life in his keeping to the last, that he could spare a breathing-place for a friend. He meant friendship, and meant nothing else, and stood by it without the slightest abatement; not veering as a weather-cock with each shift of a friend's fortune, nor like those who bury their early friendships, in order to make room for fresh corpses."

It is, therefore, impossible to sketch him

by himself. He could have said, with Ellery Channing, —

> "O band of Friends, ye breathe within this space,
> And the rough finish of a humble man
> By your kind touches rises into art."

His earliest companion was his brother John, "a flowing generous spirit," as one described him, for whom his younger brother never ceased to grieve. Walking among the Cohasset rocks and looking at the scores of shipwrecked men from the Irish brig St. John, in 1849, he said, "A man can attend but one funeral in his life, can behold but one corpse." With him it was the funeral of John Thoreau in February, 1842. They had made the voyage of the Concord and Merrimac together, in 1839; they had walked and labored together, and invented Indian names for one another from boyhood. John was "Sachem Hopeful of Hopewell," — a sunny soul, always serene and loving. When publishing his first book, in 1849, Henry dedicated it to this brother, with the simple verse —

> "Where'er thou sail'st who sailed with me,
> Though now thou climbest loftier mounts,
> And fairer rivers dost ascend,
> Be thou my Muse, my Brother John."

John Thoreau's death was singular and painful; his brother could not speak of it without physical suffering, so that when he related it to his friend Ricketson at New Bedford, he turned pale and was forced to go to the door for air. This was the only time Mr. Ricketson ever saw him show deep emotion. His sister Sophia once said:—

"Henry rarely spoke of dear John; it pained him too much. He sent the following verses from Staten Island in May, 1843, the year after John's death, in a letter to Helen. You will see that they apply to himself:"—

"Brother, where dost thou dwell?
What sun shines for thee now?
Dost thou, indeed, fare well,
As we wished here below?

"What season didst thou find?
'T was winter here.
Are not the Fates more kind
Than they appear?

"Is thy brow clear again,
As in thy youthful years?
And was that ugly pain
The summit of thy fears?

"Yet thou wast cheery still;
They could not quench thy fire;
Thou didst abide their will,
And then retire.

"Where chiefly shall I look
To feel thy presence near?
Along the neighboring brook
May I thy voice still hear?

"Dost thou still haunt the brink
Of yonder river's tide?
And may I ever think
That thou art by my side?

"What bird wilt thou employ
To bring me word of thee?
For it would give them joy,—
'T would give them liberty,
To serve their former lord
With wing and minstrelsy.

"A sadder strain mixed with their song,
They 've slowlier built their nests;
Since thou art gone
Their lively labor rests.

"Where is the finch, the thrush
I used to hear?
Ah, they could well abide
The dying year.

"Now they no more return,
I hear them not;
They have remained to mourn;
Or else forgot."

Before the death of his brother, Thoreau had formed the friendship with Ellery

Channing, that was in some degree to replace the daily intimacy he had enjoyed with John Thoreau. This man of genius, and of the moods that sometimes make genius an unhappy boon, was a year younger than Thoreau when he came, in 1841, to dwell in Concord with his bride, a younger sister of Margaret Fuller. They lived first in a cottage near Mr. Emerson's, Thoreau being at that time an inmate of Mr. Emerson's household; afterwards, in 1843, Mr. Channing removed to a hill-top some miles away, then to New York in 1844–45, then to Europe for a few months, and finally to a house on the main street of the village, opposite the last residence of the Thoreau family, where Henry lived from 1850 till his death in 1862. In the garden of Mr. Channing's house, which lay on the river, Thoreau kept his boat, under a group of willows, and from that friendly harbor all his later voyages were made. At times they talked of occupying this house together.

"I have an old house and a garden patch," said Channing, "you have legs and arms, and we both need each other's companionship. These miserable cracks and crannies which have made the wall of life look thin and fungus-like, will be cemented by the sweet and solid mortar of friendship."

They did in fact associate more closely than if they had lived in the same house.

At the age of thirty-eight, when contemplating a removal from the neighborhood of his friend Thoreau, this humorous man of letters thus described himself and his tastes to another friend: —

"I am a poet, or of a poetical temper or mood, with a very limited income both of brains and of moneys. This world is rather a sour world. But as I am, equally with you, an admirer of Cowper, why should I not prove a sort of unnecessary addition to your neighborhood possibly? I may leave Concord, and my aim would be to get a small place, in the vicinity of a large town, with some land, and, if possible, near to some *one* person with whom I might in some measure fraternize. Come, my neighbor! thou hast now a new occupation, the setting up of a poet and literary man, — one who loves old books, old garrets, old wines, old pipes, and (last not least) Cowper. We might pass the winter in comparing *variorum* editions of our favorite authors, and the summer in walking and horticulture. This is a grand scheme of life. All it requires is the house of which I spake. I think one in middle life feels averse to change, and especially to local change. The Lares and Penates love to establish themselves, and desire no moving. But the fatal hour may come, when, bidding one long, one last adieu to those weather-beaten Penates, we sally forth with Don Quixote, once more to strike our lances into some new truth, or life, or man."

This hour did come, and the removal was made for a few months or years, during which the two friends met at odd intervals, and in queer companionship. But the "sweet and solid mortar of friendship" was never broken, though the wall of life came to look like a ruin. When, in Thoreau's last illness, Channing, in deep grief, said "that a change had come over the dream of life, and that solitude began to peer out curiously from the dells and wood-roads," Thoreau whispered, "with his foot on the step of the other world," says Channing, "It is better some things should end." Of their earlier friendship, and of Channing's poetic gift, so admirable, yet so little appreciated by his contemporaries, this mention occurs in a letter written by Thoreau in March, 1856: —

"I was surprised to hear the other day that Channing was in X. When he was here last (in December, I think), he said, like himself, in answer to my inquiry where he lived, 'that he did not know the name of the place;' so it has remained in a degree of obscurity to me. I am rejoiced to hear that you are getting on so bravely with him and his verses. He and I, as you know, have been old cronies,—

"'Fed the same flock, by fountain, shade, and rill,
Together both, ere the high lawns appeared
Under the opening eyelids of the morn,
We drove afield, and both together heared,' etc.

"'But O, the heavy change,' now he is gone. The Channing you have seen and described is the real Simon Pure. You have seen him. Many a good ramble may you have together! You will see in him still more of the same kind to attract and to puzzle you. How to serve him most effectually has long been a problem with his friends. Perhaps it is left for you to solve it. I suspect that the most that you or any one can do for him is to appreciate his genius,—to buy and read, and cause others to buy and read his poems. That is the hand which he has put forth to the world,—take hold of that. Review them if you can,—perhaps take the risk of publishing something more which he may write. Your knowledge of Cowper will help you to know Channing. He will accept sympathy and aid, but he will not bear questioning, unless the aspects of the sky are particularly auspicious. He will ever be 'reserved and enigmatic,' and you must deal with him at arm's length. I have no secrets to tell you concerning him, and do not wish to call obvious excellences and defects by far-fetched names. Nor need I suggest how witty and poetic he is, — and what an inexhaustible fund of good-fellowship you will find in him."

In the record of his winter visitors at Walden, Thoreau had earlier made mention of Channing, who then lived on Ponkawtasset Hill, two or three miles away from the hermitage.

"He who came from farthest to my lodge," says Thoreau, "through deepest snows and most dismal tempests, was a poet. A farmer, a hunter, a soldier, a reporter, even a philosopher may be daunted, but nothing can deter a poet, for he is actuated by pure love. Who can predict his comings and goings? His business calls him out at all hours; even when doctors sleep. We made that small house ring with boisterous mirth, and resound with the murmur of much sober talk, — making amends then to Walden vale for the long silences. At suitable intervals there were regular salutes of laughter, which might have been referred indifferently to the last uttered or the forthcoming jest."

In his "Week," as Thoreau floats down the Concord, past the Old Manse, he commemorates first Hawthorne and then Channing, saying of the latter, —

"On Ponkawtasset, since, with such delay,
Down this still stream we took our meadowy way,
A poet wise hath settled whose fine ray
Doth faintly shine on Concord's twilight day.
Like those first stars, whose silver beams on high,
Shining more brightly as the day goes by,
Most travelers cannot at first descry,
But eyes that wont to range the evening sky."

These were true and deserved compliments, but they availed little (no more than did the praises of Emerson in the "Dial," and of Hawthorne in his "Mosses") to make Channing known to the general reader. Some years after Thoreau's death, when writing to another friend, this neglected poet said: —

"Is there no way of disabusing S. of the liking he has for the verses I used to write? You probably know he is my only patron, but that is no reason he should be led astray. *There is no other test* of the value of poetry, but its popularity. My verses have never secured a single reader but S. He really believes, I think, in those so-called verses; but they are not good,— they are wholly unknown and unread, and always will be. Mediocre poetry is worse than nothing, — and mine is not even mediocre. I have presented S. with the last set of those little books there is, to have them bound, if he will. He can keep them as a literary *curio*, and in his old age amuse himself with thinking, 'How could ever I have liked these?'"

Yet this self-disparaging poet was he who wrote,—

"If my bark sinks, 't is to another sea,"—

and who cried to his companions,—

"Ye heavy-hearted mariners
Who sail this shore,—
Ye patient, ye who labor,
Sitting at the sweeping oar,
And see afar the flashing sea-gulls play
On the free waters, and the glad bright day
Twine with his hand the spray,—
From out your dreariness,
From your heart-weariness,
I speak, for I am yours
On these gray shores."

It is he, also, who has best told, in prose and verse, what Thoreau was in his character and his literary art. In dedicating to his friend Henry, the poem called "Near Home," published in 1858, Channing thus addressed him: —

> "Modest and mild and kind,
> Who never spurned the needing from thy door —
> (Door of thy heart, which is a palace-gate);
> Temperate and faithful, — in whose word the world
> Might trust, sure to repay; unvexed by care,
> Unawed by Fortune's nod, slave to no lord,
> Nor coward to thy peers, — long shalt thou live!
> Not in this feeble verse, this sleeping age, —
> But in the roll of Heaven, and at the bar
> Of that high court where Virtue is in place,
> There thou shalt fitly rule, and read the laws
> Of that supremer state, — writ Jove's behest,
> And even old Saturn's chronicle;
> Works ne'er Hesiod saw, — types of all things,
> And portraitures of all — whose golden leaves,
> Roll back the ages' doors, and summon up
> Unsleeping truths, by which wheels on Heaven's prime."

In these majestic lines, suggestive of Dante, of Shakespeare, and of Milton, yet fitting, by the force of imagination, to the simplicity and magnanimity that Thoreau had displayed, one reads the secret of that character which made the Concord recluse first declare to the world the true mission of John Brown, whose friend he had been for a few years. Of Alcott and of Hawthorne, of Margaret Fuller and Horace Greeley, he had been longer the friend; and in the year before he met Brown he had stood face to face with Walt Whitman in Brooklyn. Mr. Alcott's testimony to Thoreau's worth and friendliness has been constant.

"If I were to proffer my earnest prayer to the gods for the greatest of all human privileges," he said one day, after returning from an evening spent at Walden with Thoreau, "it should be for the gift of a severely candid friend. To most, the presence of such is painfully irksome; they are lovers of present reputation, and not of that exaltation of soul which friends and discourse were given to awaken and cherish in us. Intercourse of this kind I have found possible with my friends Emerson and Thoreau; and the evenings passed in their society during these winter months have realized my conception of what friendship, when great and genuine, owes to and takes from its objects."

Not less emphatic was Thoreau's praise of Mr. Alcott, after these long winter evenings with him in the hut: —

"One of the last of the philosophers," he writes in "Walden," — "Connecticut gave him to the world, — he peddled first her wares, afterwards, as he declares, his brains. These he peddles still, prompting God and disgracing man, bearing for fruit his brain only, like the nut its kernel. I think he must be the man of the most faith of any alive. His words and attitude always suppose a better state of things than other men are acquainted with, and he will be the last man to be disappointed as the ages revolve. He has no venture in the present. But though comparatively disregarded now, laws unsuspected by most will take effect, and masters of families and rulers will come to him for advice. A true friend of man: almost the only friend of human progress. He is perhaps the sanest man and has the fewest crotchets of any I chance to know, — the same yesterday, to-day, and to-morrow. Of yore we had sauntered and talked, and effectually put the world behind us; for he was pledged to no institution in it, freeborn, *ingenuus*. Great Looker! great Expecter! to converse with whom was a New England Night's Entertainment. Ah! such discourse we had, hermit and philosopher, and the old settler I have spoken of, — we three, — it expanded and racked my little house."

Nor did Thoreau participate in such discourse at Walden alone, but frequented Mr. Alcott's conversations at Mr. Emerson's house in Concord, at Hawthorne's in Salem, at Marston Watson's in Plymouth, at Daniel Ricketson's in New Bedford, and once or twice in Boston and New York. With Mr. Alcott and Alice Carey, Thoreau visited Horace Greeley at Chappaqua, in 1856, and with Mr. Alcott alone he called on Walt Whitman in Brooklyn the same year.

Between Hawthorne and Thoreau, Ellery Channing was perhaps the interpreter, for they had not very much in common, though friendly and mutually respectful. The boat in which Thoreau made his voyage of 1839, on the Concord and Merrimac, came afterwards into Hawthorne's possession, and was the frequent vehicle for Channing and Hawthorne as they made those excursions which Hawthorne has commemorated. Channing also has commemorated those years when Hawthorne spent the happiest hours of his life in the Old Manse, to which he had removed soon after his marriage in 1842: —

"There in the old gray house, whose end we see
Half peeping through the golden willow's veil,
Whose graceful twigs make foliage through the year,
My Hawthorne dwelt, a scholar of rare worth,
The gentlest man that kindly nature drew;

New England's Chaucer, Hawthorne fitly lives.
His tall, compacted figure, ably strung
To urge the Indian chase or guide the way,
Softly reclining 'neath the aged elm,
Like some still rock looked out upon the scene,
As much a part of nature as itself."

In July, 1860, writing to his sister Sophia, among the New Hampshire mountains, Thoreau said: —

"Mr. Hawthorne has come home. I went to meet him the other evening (at Mr. Emerson's), and found that he had not altered, except that he was looking pretty brown after his voyage. He is as simple and childlike as ever."

This was upon the return of Hawthorne from his long residence abroad, in England, Portugal, and Italy. Thoreau died two years before Hawthorne, and they are buried within a few feet of each other in the Concord cemetery, their funerals having proceeded from the same parish church near by.

Of Thoreau's relations with Emerson, this is not the place to speak in full; it was, however, the most important, if not the most intimate, of all his friendships, and that out of which the others mainly grew. Their close acquaintance began in 1837. In the latter part of April, 1841, Thoreau became an inmate of Mr. Emerson's house, and remained there till, in the spring of 1843, he went for a few months to be the tutor of Mr. William Emerson's sons at Staten Island. In 1840, while teaching school in Concord, Thoreau seems to have been fully admitted into that circle of which Emerson, Alcott, and Margaret Fuller were the leaders. In May, 1840, this circle met, as it then did frequently, at the house of Mr. Emerson, to converse on "the inspiration of the Prophet and Bard, the nature of Poetry, and the causes of the sterility of Poetic Inspiration in our age and country." Mr. Alcott. in his diary, has preserved a record of this meeting, and some others of the same kind. It seems that on this occasion — Thoreau being not quite twenty-three years old, Mr. Alcott forty-one, Mr. Emerson thirty-seven, and Miss Fuller thirty — all these were present, and also Jones Very, the Salem poet, Dr. F. H. Hedge, Dr. C. A. Bartol, Dr. Caleb Stetson, and Robert Bartlett of Plymouth. Bartlett and Very were graduates of Harvard a year before Thoreau, and afterwards tutors there; indeed, all the company except Alcott were Cambridge scholars, — for Margaret Fuller, without entering college, had breathed in the learned air of Cambridge, and gone beyond the students who were her companions. I find no earlier record of Thoreau's participation in these meetings; but afterward he was often present. In May, 1839, Mr. Alcott had held one of his conversations at the house of Thoreau's mother, but no mention is made of Henry taking part in it. At a conversation in Concord in 1846, one April evening, Thoreau came in from his Walden hermitage, and protested with some vehemence against Mr. Alcott's declaration that Jesus "stood in a more tender and intimate nearness to the heart of mankind than any character in life or literature." Thoreau thought he "asserted this claim for the fair Hebrew in exaggeration"; yet he could say in the "Week," "It is necessary not to be Christian to appreciate the beauty and significance of the life of Christ."

This earliest of his volumes, like most of his writings, is a record of his friendships, and in it we find that high-toned, paradoxical essay on Love and Friendship, which has already been quoted. To read this literally, as Channing says, "would be to accuse him of stupidity; he gossips there of a high, imaginary world." But its tone is no higher than was the habitual feeling of Thoreau towards his friends, or that sentiment which he inspired in them. In Mr. Alcott's diary for March 16, 1847, he writes, two years before the "Week" was made public: —

"This evening I pass with Thoreau at his hermitage on Walden, and he reads me some passages from his manuscript volume, entitled 'A Week on the Concord and Merrimac Rivers.' The book is purely American, fragrant with the life of New England woods and streams, and could have been written nowhere else. Especially am I touched by his sufficiency and soundness, his aboriginal vigor, — as if a man had once more come into Nature who knew what Nature meant him to do with her, — Virgil, and White of Selborne, and Izaak Walton, and Yankee settler all in one. I came home at midnight, through the woody snow-paths, and slept with the pleasing dream that presently the press would give me two books to be proud of — Emerson's 'Poems,' and Thoreau's 'Week.'"

This high anticipation of the young author's career was fully shared by Emerson himself, who everywhere praised the genius of Thoreau; and when in England in 1848, listened readily to a proposition from Dr. Chapman the publisher, for a new magazine to be called "The Atlantic," and printed at the same time in London and in Boston, whose chief contributors in England should be Froude, Garth Wilkinson, Arthur Hugh Clough, and perhaps Carlyle; and in New England, Emerson, Thoreau, Alcott, the Channings, Theodore Parker, and Elliott Cabot. The plan came to nothing, but it may have been some reminiscence of it which, nine years afterward, gave its name to that Boston magazine, the "Atlantic Monthly." Mr. Emerson's letter was dated in London, April 20, 1848, and said: —

"I find Chapman very anxious to publish a journal common to Old and New England, as was long ago proposed. Froude and Clough and other Oxonians would gladly conspire. Let the 'Massachusetts Quarterly' give place to this, and we should have two legs, and bestride the sea. Here I know so many good-minded people that I am sure will gladly combine. But what do I, or does any friend of mine in America care for a journal? Not enough, I fear, to secure an energetic work on that side. I have a letter from Cabot lately and do write him to-day. 'T is certain the Massachusetts 'Quarterly Review' will fail, unless Henry Thoreau, and Alcott, and Channing and Newcome, the fourfold visages, fly to the rescue. I am sorry that Alcott's editor, the Dumont of our Bentham, the Baruch of our Jeremiah, is so slow to be born."

In 1846, before Mr. Emerson went abroad, we find Thoreau (whose own hut beside Walden had been built and inhabited for a year) sketching a design for a lodge which Mr. Emerson then proposed to build on the opposite shore. It was to be a retreat for study and writing, at the summit of a ledge, with a commanding prospect over the level country, towards Monadnoc and Wachusett in the west and northwest. For this lookout Mr. Alcott added a story to Thoreau's sketch; but the hermitage was never built, and the plan finally resulted in a rustic summer-house, erected by Alcott with some aid from Thoreau, in Mr. Emerson's garden, in 1847–48.[1]

[1] In building this quaint structure, Thoreau was so

Humbler friends than poets and philosophers sometimes shared the companionship of these brethren in Concord. In February, 1847, Mr. Alcott, who was then a woodman, laboring on his hillside with his own axe, where afterwards Hawthorne wandered and mused, thus notes in his diary an incident not unusual in the town: —

"Our friend the fugitive, who has shared now a week's hospitalities with us (sawing and piling my wood), feels this new trust of Freedom yet unsafe here in New England, and so has left us this morning for Canada. We supplied him with the means of journeying, and bade him God-speed to a freer land. His stay with us has given image and a name to the dire entity of slavery."

It was this slave, no doubt, who had lodged for a while in Thoreau's Walden hut.

My own acquaintance with Thoreau did not begin with our common hostility to slavery, which afterwards brought us most closely together, but sprang from the ac-

averse to Mr. Alcott's plan of putting up and tearing down with no settled design of form on paper, that he withdrew his mechanic hand, so skillful in all carpenter work.

cident of my editing for a few weeks the "Harvard Magazine," a college monthly, in 1854–55, in which appeared a long review of "Walden" and the "Week." In acknowledgment of this review, which was laudatory and made many quotations from his two volumes, Thoreau, whom I had never seen, called at my room in Holworthy Hall, Cambridge, in January, 1855, and left there in my absence, a copy of the "Week" with a message implying it was for the writer of the magazine article. It so happened that I was in the College Library when Thoreau was calling on me, and when he came, directly after, to the Library, some one present pointed him out to me as the author of "Walden." I was then a senior in college, and soon to go on my winter vacation; in course of which I wrote to Thoreau from my native town, as follows: —

"HAMPTON FALLS, N. H., *Jan'y* 30th, '55.

"MY DEAR SIR, — I have had it in mind to write you a letter ever since the day when you visited me, without my knowing it, at Cambridge. I saw you afterward at the Library, but refrained from introducing myself to you, in the hope that

I should see you later in the day. But as I did not, will you allow me to seek you out, when next I come to Concord?

"The author of the criticism in the 'Harvard Magazine' is Mr. Morton of Plymouth, a friend and pupil of your friend, Marston Watson, of that old town. Accordingly I gave him the book which you left with me, judging that it belonged to him. He received it with delight, as a gift of value in itself, and the more valuable for the sake of the giver.

"We who at Cambridge look toward Concord as a sort of Mecca for our pilgrimages, are glad to see that your last book finds such favor with the public. It has made its way where your name has rarely been heard before, and the inquiry, 'Who is Mr. Thoreau?' proves that the book has in part done its work. For my own part, I thank you for the new light it shows me the aspects of Nature in, and for the marvelous beauty of your descriptions. At the same time, if any one should ask me what I think of your philosophy, I should be apt to answer that it is not worth a straw. Whenever again you visit Cambridge, be assured, sir, that it would give me much pleasure to see you at my room. There, or in Concord, I hope soon to see you; if I may intrude so much on your time.

"Believe me always, yours very truly,

"F. B. Sanborn."

This note, which I had entirely forgotten, and of which I trust my friend soon forgave the pertness, came to me recently among his papers; with one exception, it is the only letter that passed between us, I think, in an acquaintance of more than seven years. Some six weeks after its date, I went to live in Concord, and happened to take rooms in Mr. Channing's house, just across the way from Thoreau's. I met him more than once in March, 1855, but he did not call on my sister and me until the 11th of April, when I made the following brief note of his appearance: —

"To-night we had a call from Mr. Thoreau, who came at eight and stayed till ten. He talked about Latin and Greek — which he thought ought to be studied — and about other things. In his tones and gestures he seemed to me to imitate Emerson, so that it was annoying to listen to him, though he said many good things. He looks like Emerson, too, — coarser, but with something of that serenity and sagacity which E. has. Thoreau looks eminently *sagacious* — like a sort of wise, wild beast. He dresses plainly, wears a beard in his throat, and has a brown complexion."

A month or two later my diary expanded this sketch a little, with other particulars: —

"He is a little under size, with a huge Emersonian nose, bluish gray eyes, brown hair, and a ruddy weather-beaten face, which reminds me of some shrewd and honest animal's — some retired philosophical woodchuck or magnanimous fox. He dresses very plainly, wears his collar turned over like Mr. Emerson" [we young collegians then wearing ours upright], "and often an old dress-coat, broad in the skirts, and by no means a fit. He walks about with a brisk, rustic air, and never seems tired."

Notwithstanding the slow admiration that these trivial comments indicated, our friendship grew apace, and for two years or more I dined with him almost daily, and often joined in his walks and river voyages, or swam with him in some of our numerous Concord waters. In 1857 I introduced John Brown to him, then a guest at my house; and in 1859, the evening before Brown's last birthday, we listened together to the old captain's last speech in the Concord Town Hall. The events of that year and the next brought us closely together, and I found him the stanchest of friends.

This chapter might easily be extended into a volume, so long was the list of his companions, and so intimate and perfect his relation with them, at least on his own side.

"A truth-speaker he," said Emerson at his funeral, "capable of the most deep and strict conversation; a physician to the wounds of any soul; a friend, knowing not only the secret of friendship, but almost worshipped by those few persons who resorted to him as their confessor and prophet, and knew the deep value of his mind and great heart. His soul was made for the noblest society; he had in a short life exhausted the capabilities of this world; wherever there is knowledge, wherever there is virtue, wherever there is beauty, he will find a home."

CHAPTER VIII.

THE WALDEN HERMITAGE.

It is by his two years' encampment on the shore of a small lake in the Walden woods, a mile south of Concord village, that Thoreau is best known to the world; and the book which relates how he lived and what he saw there is still, as it always was, the most popular of his writings. Like all his books, it contains much that might as well have been written on any other subject; but it also describes charmingly the scenes and events of his sylvan life, — his days and nights with Nature. He spent two years and a half in this retreat, though often coming forth from it.

The localities of Concord which Thoreau immortalized were chiefly those in the neighborhood of some lake or stream, — though it would be hard to find in that well-watered town, especially in springtime, any place which is not neighbor either to the nine-times circling river Musketaquid, to the swifter Assabet,

> "That like an arrowe clear
> Through Troy rennest aie downward to the sea," —

to Walden or White Pond, to Bateman's Pond, to the Mill Brook, the Sanguinetto, the Nut-Meadow, or the Second Division Brook. All these waters and more are renowned again and again in Thoreau's books. Like Icarus, the ancient high-flyer, he tried his fortune upon many a river, fiord, streamlet, and broad sea, —

> "Where still the shore his brave attempt resounds."

He gave beauty and dignity to obscure places by his mention of them; and it is curious that the neighborhood of Walden, — now the most romantic and poetical region of Concord, associated in every mind with this tender lover of Nature, and his worship of her, — was anciently a place of dark repute, the home of pariahs and lawless characters, such as fringed the sober garment of many a New England village in Puritanic times.

Close by Walden is Brister's Hill, where, in the early days of emancipation in Massachusetts, the newly freed slaves of Concord magnates took up their abode, —

> "The wrathful kings on cairns apart,"

as Ossian says. Here dwelt Cato Ingraham, freedman of 'Squire Duncan Ingraham, who, when yet a slave in his master's back-yard, on the day of Concord fight, was brought to a halt by the fierce Major Pitcairn, then something the worse for 'Squire Ingraham's wine, and ordered to "lay down his arms and disperse," as the rebels at Lexington had been six hours earlier. Here also abode Zilpha, a black Circe, who spun linen, and made the Walden Woods resound with her shrill singing: —

> "Dives inaccessos ubi Solis filia lucos
> Assiduo resonat cantu, tectisque superbis
> Urit odoratam nocturna in lumina cedrum,
> Arguto tenues percurrens pectine telas."

But some paroled English prisoners in the War of 1812, burnt down her proud abode, with its imprisoned cat and dog and hens, while Zilpha was absent. Down the road towards the village from Cato's farm and Zilpha's musical loom and wheel, lived Brister Freeman, who gave his name to the hill, — Scipio Brister, "a handy negro," once the slave of 'Squire Cummings, but long since emancipated, and in Thoreau's boyhood set free again by death, and buried in an old Lincoln graveyard, near the ancestor of President Garfield, but still nearer the unmarked graves of British grenadiers, who fell in the retreat from Concord. With this Scipio Africanus Brister Libertinus, in the edge of the Walden Woods, "dwelt Fenda, his hospitable wife, who told fortunes, yet pleasantly — large, round, and black, — such a dusky orb has never rose on Concord, before or since," says Thoreau. Such was the African colony on the south side of Concord village among the woods, while on the northern edge of the village, along the Great Meadows, there dwelt another colony, headed by Cæsar Robbins, whose descendants still flit about the town. Older than all was the illustrious Guinea negro, John Jack, once a slave on the farm which is now the glebe of the Old Manse, but who purchased his freedom about the time the Old Manse was built in 1765–66. He survives in his quaint epitaph, written by Daniel Bliss, the young Tory brother of the first mistress of the manse (Mrs. William Emerson, grandmother of Emerson, the poet): —

" *God wills us free, Man wills us slaves,*
I will as God wills: God's will be done.

Here lies the body of
JOHN JACK,
A native of Africa, who died
March, 1773, aged about sixty years.
Though born in a land of slavery,
He was born free;
Though he lived in a land of liberty,
He lived a slave;
Till by his honest though stolen labors
He acquired the source of slavery
Which gave him his freedom;
Though not long before
Death the grand tyrant
Gave him his final emancipation,
And put him on a footing with kings.
Though a slave to vice,
He practised those virtues
Without which kings are but slaves."

This epitaph, and the anecdote already given concerning Cæsar Robbins, may illustrate the humanity and humor with which the freedmen of Concord were regarded, while an adventure of Scipio Brister's, in his early days of freedom, may show the mixture of savage fun and contempt that also followed them, and which some of their conduct may have deserved.

The village drover and butcher once had a ferocious bull to kill, and when he had succeeded with some difficulty in driving him into his slaughter-house, on the Walden road, nobody was willing to go in and kill him. Just then Brister Freeman, from his hill near Walden, came along the road, and was slyly invited by the butcher to go into the slaughter-house for an axe,—being told that when he brought it he should have a job to do. The unsuspecting freedman opened the door and walked in; it was shut behind him, and he found the bull drawn up in line of battle before him. After some pursuit and retreat in the narrow arena, Brister spied the axe he wanted, and began attacking his pursuer, giving him a blow here or there as he had opportunity. His employers outside watched the bull-fight through a hole in the building, and cheered on the matador with shouts and laughter. At length, by a fortunate stroke, the African conquered, the bull fell, and his slayer threw down the axe and rushed forth unhurt. But his tormentors declared "he was no longer the dim, sombre negro he went in, but literally white with terror, and what was once his wool straightened out and standing erect on his head." Without waiting to be identified, or to receive pay for his work, Brister, affrighted and wrathful, withdrew to the wooded hill and to the companionship of his fortune-telling Fenda, who had not foreseen the hazard of her spouse.

It was along the same road and down this hill, passing by the town "poor-farm" and poor-house, — the last retreat of these straggling soldiers of fortune, — that Thoreau went toward the village jail from his hermitage, that day in 1846, when the town constable carried him off from the shoemaker's to whose shop he had gone to get a cobbled shoe. His room-mate in jail for the single night he slept there, was introduced to him by the jailer, Mr. Staples (a real name), as "a first-rate fellow and a clever man," and on being asked by Thoreau why he was in prison, replied, "Why, they accuse me of burning a barn, but I never did it." As near as Thoreau could make out, he had gone to bed in a barn when drunk, and smoked his pipe there. Such were the former denizens of the Walden woods — votaries of Bacchus and Apollo, and extremely liable to take fire upon small occasion, — like Giordano Bruno's sonneteer, who, addressing the Arabian Phenix, says, —

> "*Tu bruci 'n un, ed io in ogni loco,*
> *Io da Cupido, hai tu da Febo il foco.*"

It seems by the letter of Margaret Fuller in 1841 (cited in chapter VI.), that Thoreau had for years meditated a withdrawal to a solitary life. The retreat he then had in view was, doubtless, the Hollowell Farm, a place, as he says, "of complete retirement, being about two miles from the village, half a mile from the nearest neighbor, and separated from the highway by a broad field." The house stood apart from the road to Nine-Acre Corner, fronting the Musketaquid on a green hill-side, and was first seen by Thoreau as a boy, in his earliest voyages up the river to Fairhaven Bay, "concealed behind a dense grove of red maples, through which I heard the house-dog bark." This place Thoreau once bought, but released it to the owner, whose wife refused to sign the deed of sale. In his Walden venture he was a squatter, using for his house-lot a woodland of Mr. Emerson's, who, for the sake of his walks and his wood-fire, had bought land on both sides of Walden Pond.

How early Thoreau formed his plan of retiring to a hut among these woods, I have not learned; but in a letter written to him March 5, 1845, by his friend Channing, a passage occurs concerning it; and it was in the latter part of the same month that Thoreau borrowed Mr. Alcott's axe and went across the fields to cut the timber for his cabin. Channing writes: —

"I see nothing for you in this earth but that field which I once christened 'Briars;' go out upon that, build yourself a hut, and there begin the grand process of devouring yourself alive. I see no alternative, no other hope for you. Eat yourself up; you will eat nobody else, nor anything else. Concord is just as good a place as any other; there are, indeed, more people in the streets of that village than in the streets of this." [He was writing from the Tribune Office, in

New York.] "This is a singularly muddy town; muddy, solitary, and silent. I saw Teufelsdröckh a few days since; he said a few words to me about you. Says he, 'That fellow Thoreau might be something, if he would only take a journey through the Everlasting No, thence for the North Pole. By G—,' said the old clothes-bag, warming up, 'I should like to take that fellow out into the Everlasting No, and explode him like a bombshell; he would make a loud report; it would be fun to see him pick himself up. He needs the Blumine flower business; that would be his salvation. He is too dry, too composed, too chalky, too concrete. Does that execrable compound of sawdust and stagnation L. still prose about nothing? and that nutmeg-grater of a Z. yet shriek about nothing? Does anybody still think of coming to Concord to live? I mean new people? If they do, let them beware of you philosophers.'"

Of course, this imaginary Teufelsdröckh, like Carlyle's, was the satirical man in the writer himself, suggesting the humorous and contradictory side of things, and glancing at the coolness of Thoreau, which his friends sometimes found provoking. In his own person Channing adds:—

"I should be pleased to hear from Kamchatka

occasionally; my last advices from the Polar Bear are getting stale. In addition to this I find that my corresponding members at Van Diemen's Land have wandered into limbo. I hear occasionally from the World; everything seems to be promising in that quarter; business is flourishing, and the people are in good spirits. I feel convinced that the Earth has less claims to our regard than formerly; these mild winters deserve severe censure. But I am well aware that the Earth will talk about the necessity of routine, taxes, etc. On the whole it is best not to complain without necessity."

It is well to read this shrewd humor, uttered in the opposite sense from Thoreau's paradoxical wit in his "Walden," as an introduction or motto to that book. For Thoreau has been falsely judged from the wit and the paradox of "Walden," as if he were a hater of men, or foolishly desired all mankind to retire to the woods. As Channing said, soon after his friend's death, —

"The fact that our author lived for a while alone in a shanty, near a pond, and named one of his books after the place where it stood, has led some to say he was a barbarian or a misanthrope. It was a writing-case; here in this wooden inkstand he wrote a good part of his famous 'Walden,' and this solitary woodland pool was more to his Muse than all oceans of the planet, by the force of imagination. Some have fancied, because he moved to Walden, he left his family. He bivouacked there and really lived at home, where he went every day."

This last is not literally true, for he was sometimes secluded in his hut for days together; but he remained as social at Walden as he had been while an inmate of Mr. Emerson's family in 1841–43, or again in 1847–48, after giving up his hermitage. He, in fact, as he says himself, —

"Went to the woods because he wished to live deliberately, to front only the essential facts of life, and see if he could not learn what it had to teach, and not, when he came to die, discover that he had not lived."

In another place he says he went to Walden to "transact some private business," and this he did to good purpose. He edited there his "Week," some portions of which had appeared in the "Dial" from 1840 to 1844, but which was not published as a volume until 1849, although he had made many attempts to issue it earlier. It was at Walden, also, that he wrote his essay on Carlyle, which was first published in "Graham's Magazine," at Philadelphia, in 1847, through the good offices of Horace Greeley, of which we shall hear more in the next chapter.

Thoreau's hermit life was not, then, merely a protest against the luxury and the restraints of society, nor yet an austere discipline such as monks and saints have imposed upon themselves for their souls' good. "My purpose in going to Walden was not to live cheaply, nor to live dearly there, but to transact some private business with the fewest obstacles." He lived a life of labor and study in his hut. Emerson says, "as soon as he had exhausted the advantages of that solitude, he abandoned it." He had edited his first book there; had satisfied himself that he was fit to be an author, and had passed his first examinations; then he graduated from that gymnasium as another young student might from the medical college or the polytechnic school. "I left the woods for as good a reason as I went there." His abandoned hut was then taken by a Scotch gardener, Hugh Whelan by name, who removed it some rods away, to the midst of Thoreau's bean-field, and made it his cottage for a few years. Then it was bought by a farmer, who put it on wheels and carried it three miles northward, toward the entry of the Estabrook Farm on the old Carlisle road, where it stood till after Thoreau's death, — a shelter for corn and beans, and a favorite haunt of squirrels and blue jays. The wood-cut representing the hermitage in the first edition of "Walden," is from a sketch made by Sophia Thoreau, and is more exact than that given in Page's "Life of Thoreau," but in neither picture are the trees accurately drawn.

On the spot where Thoreau lived at Walden there is now a cairn of stones, yearly visited by hundreds, and growing in height as each friend of his muse adds a stone from the shore of the fair water he loved so well.

> "Beat with thy paddle on the boat
> Midway the lake, — the wood repeats
> The ordered blow; the echoing note
> Is ended in thy ear; yet its retreats
> Conceal Time's possibilities;
> And in this Man the nature lies
> Of woods so green,
> And lakes so sheen,
> And hermitages edged between.

"And I may tell you that the Man was good,
Never did his neighbor harm, —
Sweet was it where he stood,
Sunny and warm;
Like the seat beneath a pine
That winter suns have cleared away
With their yellow tine, —
Red-cushionéd and tasseled with the day."

The events and thoughts of Thoreau's life at Walden may be read in his book of that name. As a protest against society, that life was ineffectual, — as the communities at Brook Farm and Fruitlands had proved to be; and as the Fourierite phalansteries, in which Horace Greely interested himself, were destined to be. In one sense, all these were failures; but in Thoreau's case the failure was slight, the discipline and experience gained were invaluable. He never regretted it, and the Walden episode in his career has made him better known than anything else.

CHAPTER IX.

HORACE IN THE RÔLE OF MÆCENAS.

In a letter to his sister Sophia, July 21, 1843, written from Mr. William Emerson's house at Staten Island, Thoreau says: —

"In New York I have seen, since I wrote last, Horace Greeley, editor of the 'Tribune,' who is cheerfully in earnest at his office of all work, — a hearty New Hampshire boy as one would wish to meet, — and says, 'Now be neighborly.' He believes only or mainly, first in the Sylvania Association, somewhere in Pennsylvania; and secondly, and most of all, in a new association, to go into operation soon in New Jersey, with which he is connected."

This was the "Phalanstery" at which W. H. Channing afterward preached. A fortnight later, Thoreau writes to Mr. Emerson: —

"I have had a pleasant talk with W. H. Channing; and Greeley, too, it was refreshing to meet. They were both much pleased with your criticism on Carlyle, but thought that you had overlooked what chiefly concerned them in the book, — its practical aims and merits."

This refers to the notice of Carlyle's "Past and Present," in the "Dial" for July, 1843, and shows that Mr. Greeley was a quick reader of that magazine, as Thoreau always was of the "New York Tribune." From this time onward a warm friendship continued between Thoreau and Greeley, and many letters went to and fro, which reveal the able editor in the light of a modern Mæcenas to the author of the Musketaquid Georgics.

No letters seem to have passed between them earlier than 1846; and in 1844–45 Thoreau must have known the "Tribune" editor best through his newspaper, and from the letters of Margaret Fuller, Ellery Channing, and other common friends, who saw much of him then, admired and laughed at him, or did both by turns. Miss Fuller, who had gone to New York to write for the "Tribune," and to live in its Editor's family, wrote: —

"Mr. Greeley is a man of genuine excellence, honorable, benevolent, and of an uncorrupted disposition. He is sagacious, and, in his way, of even great abilities. In modes of life and manners, he is a man of the people, — and of the American people. With the exception of my own mother, I think him the most disinterestedly generous person I have ever known."

There was a laughable side even to these fine traits, and there were eccentricities of dress and manner, which others saw more keenly than this generous woman. Ellery Channing, — whose eye no whimsical or beautiful object ever escaped, — in the letter of March, 1845, already cited, thus signaled to Thoreau the latest news of his friend: —

"Mumbo Jumbo is recovering from an attack of sore eyes, and will soon be out, in a pair of canvas trousers, scarlet jacket, and cocked hat. I understand he intends to demolish all the remaining species of Fetichism at a meal. I think it is probable it will vomit him."

Thoreau wrote an essay on Carlyle in 1846, and in the summer of that year sent it to Mr. Greeley, with a request that he would find a place for it in some magazine. To this request, which Mr. Greeley himself had invited, no doubt, he thus replied: —

"*August* 16, 1846.

"MY DEAR THOREAU, — Believe me when I say that I *mean* to do the errand you have asked of me, and that soon. But I am not sanguine of success, and have hardly a hope that it will be immediate, if ever. I hardly know a work that would publish your article all at once, and 'to be continued' are words shunned like a pestilence. But I know you have written a good thing about Carlyle, — too solidly good, I fear, to be profitable to yourself, or attractive to publishers. Did'st thou ever, O my friend! ponder on the significance and cogency of the assurance, 'Ye cannot serve God and Mammon,' as applicable to literature, — applicable, indeed, to all things whatsoever? God grant us grace to endeavor to serve Him rather than Mammon, — that ought to suffice us. In my poor judgment, if anything is calculated to make a scoundrel of an honest man, writing to sell is that very particular thing.

"Yours heartily, HORACE GREELEY.

"Remind Ralph Waldo Emerson and wife of my existence and grateful remembrance."

On the 30th of September Mr. Greeley again wrote, saying, —

"I learned to-day, through Mr. Griswold, former editor of 'Graham's Magazine,' that your lecture is accepted, to appear in that magazine.

Of course it is to be paid for at the usual rate, as I expressly so stated when I inclosed it to Graham. He has not written me a word on the subject, which induces me to think he may have written you.[1] Please write me if you would have me speak further on the subject. The pay, however, is sure, though the amount may not be large, and I think you may wait until the article appears, before making further stipulations on the subject."

From the tenor of this I infer that Thoreau had written to say that he might wish to read his "Thomas Carlyle" as a lecture, and desired to stipulate for that before it was printed. He might be excused for some solicitude concerning payment, from his recent experience with the publishers of the "Boston Miscellany," which had printed, in 1843, his "Walk to Wachusett." At the very time when Thoreau, in New York, was making Greeley's acquaintance, Mr. Emerson, in Boston, was dunning the Miscellaneous publishers, and wrote to Thoreau (July 20, 1843): —

"When I called on ——, their partner, in their absence, informed me that they could not pay

[1] No such letter appears.

you, at present, any part of their debt on account of the Boston 'Miscellany.' After much talking all the promise he could offer was, "that within a year it would probably be paid,' — a probability which certainly looks very slender. The very worst thing he said was the proposition that you should take your payment in the form of Boston Miscellanies! I shall not fail to refresh their memory at intervals."

But I cannot learn that anything came of it. Mr. Greeley, as we shall see, was a more successful collector. On the 26th of October, 1846, he continued the adventures of the wandering essay as follows: —

"MY FRIEND THOREAU, — I know you think it odd that you have not heard further, and, perhaps blame my negligence or engrossing cares, but, if so, without good reason. I have to-day received a letter from Griswold, in Philadelphia, who says: 'The article by Thoreau on Carlyle is in type, and will be paid for liberally.' 'Liberally' is quoted as an expression of Graham's. I know well the difference between a publisher's and an author's idea of what *is* 'liberally'; but I give you the best I can get as the result of three letters to Philadelphia on this subject.

"Success to you, my friend! Remind Mr. and

Mrs. Emerson of my existence, and my lively remembrance of their various kindnesses.

"Yours, very busy in our political contest,

"HORACE GREELEY."

It would seem that "Griswold" (who was Rufus W. Griswold, the biographer of Poe) and "Graham" (who was George R. Graham, the magazine publisher of Philadelphia), did not move so fast either in publication or in payment as they had led Mr. Greeley to expect; and also that Thoreau became impatient and wrote to his friend that he would withdraw the essay. Whereupon Mr. Greeley, under date of February 5, 1847, wrote thus: —

"MY DEAR THOREAU, — Although your letter only came to hand to-day, I attended to its subject yesterday, when I was in Philadelphia, on my way home from Washington. Your article is this moment in type, and will appear about the 20th inst., *as the leading article* in 'Graham's Magazine' for next month. Now don't object to this, nor be unreasonably sensitive at the delay. It is immensely more important to you that the article should appear thus (that is, if you have any literary aspirations) than it is that you should make a few dollars by issuing it in some other way. As to lecturing, you have been at perfect liberty to deliver it as a lecture a hundred times, if you had chosen, — the more the better. It is really a good thing, and I will see that Graham pays you fairly for it. But its appearance there is worth far more to you than money. I know there has been too much delay, and have done my best to obviate it. But I could not. A magazine that pays, and which it is desirable to be known as a contributor to, is always crowded with articles, and has to postpone some for others of even less merit. I do this myself with good things that I am not required to pay for.

"Thoreau, do not think hard of Graham. Do not try to stop the publication of your article. It is best as it is. But just sit down and write a like article about Emerson, which I will give you $25 for, if you cannot do better with it; then one about Hawthorne at your leisure, etc., etc. I will pay you the money for each of these articles on delivery, publish them when and how I please, leaving to you the copyright expressly. In a year or two, if you take care not to write faster than you think, you will have the material of a volume worth publishing, — and then we will see what can be done. There is a text somewhere in St. Paul — my Scriptural reading is getting rusty, — which says, 'Look not back to the things which are behind, but rather to those which are before,' etc. Commending this to your thoughtful appreciation, I am, yours, etc. HORACE GREELEY."

The Carlyle essay did appear in two numbers of "Graham's Magazine" (March and April, 1847), but alas, no payment came to hand. After waiting a year longer, Thoreau wrote to Greeley again (March 31, 1848), informing him of the delinquency of Griswold and Graham. At once, his friend replied (April 3), "It saddens and surprises me to know that your article was not paid for by Graham; and, since my honor is involved in the matter, I will see that you *are* paid, and that at no distant day." Accordingly on the 17th of May, 1848, he writes again as follows:—

"DEAR FRIEND THOREAU, — I trust you have not thought me neglectful or dilatory with regard to your business. I have done my very best, throughout, and it is only to-day that I have been able to lay my hand on the money due you from Graham. I have been to see him in Philadelphia, but did not catch him in his business office; then I have been here to meet him, and been referred to his brother, etc. I finally found the two numbers of the work in which your article was published (not easy, I assure you, for he has them not, nor his brother, and I hunted them up, and bought one of them at a very out-of-the-way place), and with these I made out a regular bill for the contribution; drew a draft on G. R. Graham for the amount, gave it to his brother here for collection, and to-day received the money. Now you see how to get pay yourself, another time; I have pioneered the way, and you can follow it easily yourself. There has been no intentional injustice on Graham's part; but he is overwhelmed with business, has too many irons in the fire, and we did not go at him the right way. Had you drawn a draft on him, at first, and given it to the Concord Bank to send in for collection, you would have received your money long since. Enough of this. I have made Graham pay you $75, but I only send you $50, for, having got so much for Carlyle, I am ashamed to take your 'Maine Woods' for $25."

This last allusion is to a new phase of the queer patronage which the good Mæcenas extended to our Concord poet. In his letter of March 31, 1848, Thoreau had offered Greeley, in compliance with his suggestion of the previous year, a paper on "Ktaadn and the Maine Woods," which afterwards appeared in the "Union Magazine." On the 17th of April Greeley writes: —

"I inclose you $25 for your article on Maine Scenery, as promised. I know it is worth more, though I have not yet found time to read it; but I have tried once to sell it without success. It is rather long for my columns, and too fine for the million; but I consider it a cheap bargain, and shall print it myself, if I do not dispose of it to better advantage. You will not, of course, consider yourself under any sort of obligation to me, for my offer was in the way of business, and I have got more than the worth of my money."

On the 17th of May he adds: —

"I have expectations of procuring it a place in a new magazine of high character that will pay. I don't expect to get as much for it as for Carlyle, but I hope to get $50. If you are satisfied to take the $25 for your 'Maine Woods,' say so, and I will send on the money; but I don't want to seem a Jew, buying your articles at half price to speculate upon. If you choose to let it go that way, it shall be so; but I would sooner do my best for you, and send you the money."

On the 28th of October, 1848, he writes:

"I break a silence of some duration to inform you that I hope on Monday to receive payment for your glorious account of 'Ktaadn and the Maine Woods,' which I bought of you at a Jew's bargain, and sold to the 'Union Magazine.' I am to get $75 for it, and, as I don't choose to *exploiter* you at such a rate, I shall insist on inclosing you $25 more in this letter, which will still leave me $25 to pay various charges and labors I have incurred in selling your articles and getting paid for them, — the latter by far the more difficult portion of the business."

In the letter of April 17, 1848, Mr. Greeley had further said: —

"If you will write me two or three articles in the course of the summer, I think I can dispose of them for your benefit. But write not more than half as long as your article just sent me, for that is too long for the magazines. If that were in two, it would be far more valuable. What about your book (the 'Week')? Is anything going on about it now? Why did not Emerson try it in England? I think the Howitts could get it favorably before the British public. If you can suggest any way wherein I can put it forward, do not hesitate, but command me."

In the letter of May 17th, he reiterates the advice to be brief: —

"Thoreau, if you will only write one or two articles, when in the spirit, about half the length of this, I can sell it readily and advantageously. The length of your papers is the only impediment to their appreciation by the magazines. Give me one or two shorter, and I will try to coin them speedily."

May 25th he returns to the charge, when sending the last twenty-five dollars for the "Maine Woods": —

"Write me something shorter when the spirit moves (never write a line otherwise, for the hack writer is a slavish beast, *I* know), and I will sell it for you soon. I want one shorter article from your pen that will be quoted, as these long articles cannot be, and let the public know something of your way of thinking and seeing. It will do good. What do you think of following out your thought in an essay on 'The Literary Life?' You need not make a personal allusion, but I know you can write an article worth reading on that theme, when you are in the vein."

After a six months' interval (November 19, 1848), Greeley resumes in a similar strain: —

"FRIEND THOREAU, — Yours of the 17th received. Say we are even on money counts, and let the matter drop. I have tried to serve you, and have been fully paid for my own disbursements and trouble in the premises. So we will move on.

"I think you will do well to send me some passages from one or both of your new works to dispose of to the magazines. This will be the best kind of advertisement, whether for a publisher or for readers. You may write with an angel's pen, yet your writings have no mercantile money value till you are known and talked of as an author. Mr. Emerson would have been twice as much known and read, if he had written for the magazines a little, just to let common people know of his existnce. I believe a chapter from one of your books printed in 'Graham,' or 'The Union,' will add many to the readers of the volume when issued. Here is the reason why British books sell so much better among us than American, — because they are thoroughly advertised through the British reviews, magazines, and journals which circulate or are copied among us. However, do as you please. If you choose to send me one of your manuscripts I will get it published, but I cannot promise you any considerable recompense; and, indeed, if Monroe will do it, that will be better. Your writings are in advance of the general mind here; Boston is nearer their standard. I never saw the verses you speak of. Wont you send them again? I have been buried up in politics for the last six weeks. Kind regards to Emerson. It is doubtful about my seeing you this season."

Here the letters ceased for a time. "Monroe did it," — that is, a Boston bookseller published Thoreau's "Week," which was favorably reviewed by George Ripley in the "Tribune," by Lowell in the "Massachusetts Quarterly," and by others elsewhere; but the book did not sell, and involved its author in debt for its printing. To meet this he took up surveying as a business, and after a time, when some payment must be made, he asked his friend Greeley for a loan. In the interval, Margaret Fuller had written from Europe those remarkable letters for the "Tribune," had married in Italy, sailed for home in 1850, and died on the shore of Fire Island, near New York, whither Thoreau went with her friends to learn her fate, and recover the loved remains. This was in July, 1850, and he no doubt saw Mr. Greeley there. A year and a half later, when he was seeking opportunities to lecture, he wrote to Mr. Greeley again, in February, 1852, offering himself to lecture in a course at New York, which the "Tribune" editor had some interest in. The reply was this: —

"NEW YORK, *February* 24, 1852.

"MY FRIEND THOREAU, — Thank you for your remembrance, though the motto you suggest is impracticable. The People's Course is full for the season; and even if it were not, your name would probably not pass; because it is not merely necessary that each lecturer should continue *well* the course, but that he shall be *known* as the very man beforehand. Whatever draws less than fifteen hundred hearers damages the finances of the movement, so low is the admission, and so large the expense. But, Thoreau, you are a better speaker than many, but a far better writer still. Do you wish to swap any of your 'wood-notes wild' for dollars? If yea, and you will sell me some articles, shorter, if you please, than the former, I will try to coin them for you. Is it a bargain? Yours,

"HORACE GREELEY."

Thoreau responded at once with some manuscripts (March 5), and was thus addressed, March 18, by his friend: —

"I shall get you some money for the articles you sent me, though not immediately. As to your long account of a Canadian tour, I don't know. It looks unmanageable. Can't you cut it into three or four, and omit all that relates to time? The cities are described to death; but I know you are at home with Nature, and that *she* rarely and slowly changes. Break this up, if you can, and I will try to have it swallowed and digested."

A week later he sent a letter from the publisher, Sartain, accepting the articles for a low price,[1] and adds: "If you break up

[1] That is to say, a low price compared with what is now paid. As the letter courteously states some matters that have now become curious, it may be given: —

"PHILADELPHIA, *March* 24, 1852.

"DEAR SIR, — I have read the articles of Mr. Thoreau forwarded by you, and will be glad to publish them if our terms are satisfactory. We generally pay for prose composition per printed page, and would allow him three dollars per page. We do not pay more than four dollars for any that we now engage. I did not suppose our maximum rate would have paid you (Mr. Greeley) for your lecture, and therefore requested to know your own terms. Of course, when an article is unusually desirable, we may deviate from rule; I now only mention ordinary arrangement. I was very sorry not to have your article, but shall enjoy the reading of it in Graham. Mr. T. might send us some further contriyour 'Excursion to Canada' into three or four articles, I have no doubt I could get it published on similar terms." April 3, 1852, he returns to a former proposition, that Thoreau shall write about Emerson as he did six years before on Carlyle.

"FRIEND THOREAU, — I wish you to write me an article on Ralph Waldo Emerson, his Works and Ways, extending to one hundred pages, or so, of letter sheet like this, to take the form of a review of his writings, but to give some idea of the Poet, the Genius, the Man, — with some idea of the New England scenery and home influence, which have combined to make him what he is. Let it be calm, searching, and impartial; nothing like adulation, but a just summing up of what he is and what he has done. I mean to get this into the 'Westminster Review,' but if not acceptable there, I will publish it elsewhere. I will pay you fifty dollars for the article when delivered; in advance, if you desire it. Say the word, and I will send the money at once. It is perfectly convenient to do so. Your 'Carlyle' article is my model, but you can give us Emerson

butions, and shall at least receive prompt and courteous decision respecting them. Yours truly,

"JOHN SARTAIN."

It seems sad so candid and amiable a publisher should not have succeeded.

better than you did Carlyle. I presume he would allow you to write extracts for this purpose from his lectures not yet published. I would delay the publication of the article to suit his publishing arrangements, should that be requested.

"Yours, HORACE GREELEY."

To this request, as before, there came a prompt negative, although Thoreau was then sadly in need of money. Mr. Greeley wrote, April 20: —

"I am rather sorry you will not do the 'Works and Ways,' but glad that you are able to employ your time to better purpose. But your Quebec notes have n't reached me yet, and I fear the 'good time' is passing. They ought to have appeared in the June number of the monthlies, but now cannot before July. If you choose to send them to me all in a lump, I will try to get them printed in that way. I don't care about them if you choose to reserve, or to print them elsewhere; but I can better make a use for them at this season that at any other."

They were sent, and offered to the "Whig Review," and to other magazines; but on the 25th of June, Mr. Greeley writes: —

"I have had only bad luck with your manuscript. Two magazines have refused it on the ground of its length, saying that articles 'To be continued' are always unpopular, however good. I will try again."

It seems that the author had relied upon money from this source, and a week or two later he asks his friend to lend him the expected seventy-five dollars, offering security, with mercantile scrupulosity. Promptly came this answer: —

"New York, *July* 8, 1852.

"Dear Thoreau, — Yours received. I was absent yesterday. I *can* lend you the seventy-five dollars, and am very glad to do it. Don't talk about security. I am sorry about your MSS., which I do not quite despair of using to your advantage. Yours, Horace Greeley."

The "Yankee in Canada," as it is now called (the record of Thoreau's journey through French Canada in September, 1850, with Ellery Channing), was offered to "Putnam's Magazine" by Mr. Greeley, and begun there, but ill-luck attended it. Before it went the paper on "Cape Cod," which became the subject of controversy, first as to price, and then as to its tone towards the people of that region. This will explain the letters of Mr. Greeley that follow: —

"NEW YORK, *November* 23, 1852.

"MY DEAR THOREAU, — I have made no bargain — none whatever — with Putnam concerning your MSS. I have indicated no price to them. I handed over the MS. because I wished it published, and presumed that was in accordance both with your interest and your wishes. And I now say to you, that if he will pay you three dollars per printed page, I think that will be very well. I have promised to write something for him myself, and shall be well satisfied with that price. Your 'Canada' is not so fresh and acceptable as if it had just been written on the strength of a last summer's trip, and I hope you will have it printed in 'Putnam's Monthly.' But I have said nothing to his folks as to price, and will not till I hear from you again. Very probably there was some misapprehension on the part of C. I presume the price now offered you is that paid to writers generally for the 'Monthly.' As to Sartain, I know his '(Union) Magazine' has broken down, but I guess he will pay you. I have seen but one of your articles printed by him, and I think the other may be reclaimed. Please address him at once."

"NEW YORK, *January* 2, 1853.

"FRIEND THOREAU, — I have yours of the 29th, and credit you $20. Pay me when and in such sums as may be convenient. I am sorry you and C. cannot agree so as to have your whole MS. printed. It will be worth nothing elsewhere after having partly appeared in Putnam's. I think it is a mistake to conceal the authorship of the several articles, making them all (so to speak) *editorial;* but *if* that is done, don't you see that the elimination of very flagrant heresies (like your defiant Pantheism) becomes a necessity? If you had withdrawn your MSS., on account of the abominable misprints in the first number, your ground would have been far more tenable.

"However, do what you will. Yours,

"HORACE GREELEY."

Thoreau did what he would, of course, and the article in Putnam came to an abrupt end. The loan made in July, 1852, was paid with interest on the 9th of March, 1853, as the following note shows: —

"NEW YORK, *March* 16, 1853.

"DEAR SIR, — I have yours of the 9th, inclosing Putnam's check for $59, making $79 in all you have paid me. I am paid in full, and this letter is your receipt in full. I don't want any pay for my 'services,' whatever they may have been. Consider me your friend who *wished* to serve you, however unsuccessfully. Don't break with C. or Putnam."

A year later, Thoreau renewed his subscription to the "Weekly Tribune," but the letter miscarried. In due time came this reply to a third letter: —

"*March* 6, 1854.

"Dear Sir, — I presume your first letter containing the $2 was robbed by our general mail robber of New Haven, who has just been sent to the State's Prison. Your second letter has probably failed to receive attention owing to a press of business. But I will make all right. You ought to have the Semi-weekly, and I shall order it sent to you one year on trial; if you choose to write me a letter or so some time, very well; if not, we will be even without that.

"Thoreau, I want you to do something on *my* urgency. I want you to collect and arrange your 'Miscellanies' and send them to me. Put in 'Ktaadn,' 'Carlyle,' 'A Winter Walk,' 'Canada,' etc., and I will try to find a publisher who will bring them out at his own risk, and (I hope) to your ultimate profit. If you have anything new to put with them, very well; but let me have about a 12mo volume whenever you can get it ready, and see if there is not something to your credit in the bank of Fortune. Yours,

"HORACE GREELEY."

In reply, Thoreau notified his friend of the early publication of "Walden," and was thus met: —

"*March* 23, 1854.

"DEAR THOREAU, — I am glad your 'Walden' is coming out. *I* shall announce it at once, whether Ticknor does or not. I am in no hurry now about your 'Miscellanies;' take your time, select your title, and prepare your articles deliberately and finally. Then, if Ticknor will give you something worth having, let him have this too; if proffering it to him is to glut your market, let it come to me. But take your time. I was only thinking you were merely waiting when you might be doing something. I referred (without naming you) to your 'Walden' experience in my lecture on 'Self-Culture,' with which I have had ever so many audiences. This episode excited much interest, and I have been repeatedly asked who it is that I refer to.

"Yours, HORACE GREELEY.

"P. S. — You must know Miss Elizabeth Hoar, whereas I hardly do. Now, I have offered to edit Margaret's works, and I want of Elizabeth a letter or memorandum of personal recollections of Margaret and her ideas. Can't you ask her to write it for me? H. G."

To the request of this postscript Thoreau attended at once, but the "Miscellanies" dwelt not in his mind, it would seem. He had now become deeply concerned about slavery, was also pursuing his studies concerning the Indians, and had little time for the collection of his published papers. A short note of April 2, 1854, closes this part of the Greeley correspondence, thus:—

"DEAR THOREAU,—Thank you for your kindness in the matter of Margaret. Pray take no further trouble; but if anything should come in your way, calculated to help me, do not forget. Yours, HORACE GREELEY."

In August, 1855, Mr. Greeley wrote to suggest that copies of "Walden" should be sent to the "Westminster Review," to "The Reasoner," 147 Fleet Street, London, to Gerald Massey, office of the "News," Edinburgh, and to "—— Wills, Esq., Dickens's Household Words," adding:—

"There is a small class in England who ought to know what you have written, and I feel sure your publishers would not throw away copies sent to these periodicals; especially if your 'Week on the Concord and Merrimac' could accompany them. Chapman, editor of the 'Westminster,' expressed surprise that your book had not been sent him, and I could find very few who had read or seen it. If a new edition should be called for, try to have it better known in Europe, but have a few copies sent to those worthy of it, at all events."

In March, 1856, Mr. Greeley opened a new correspondence with Thoreau, asking him to become the tutor of his children, and to live with him, or near him, at Chappaqua. The proposition was made in the most generous manner, and was for a time considered by Thoreau, who felt a sense of obligation as well as a sincere friendship towards the man who had believed in him and served him so seasonably in the years of his obscurity. But it resulted in nothing further than a brief visit to Mr. Greeley in the following autumn, during which, as Thoreau used to say, Mr. Alcott and Mr. Greeley went to the opera together.

CHAPTER X.

IN WOOD AND FIELD.

EXCEPT the Indians themselves, whose wood-craft he never tires of celebrating, few Americans were ever more at home in the open air than Thoreau; not even his friend John Brown, who, like himself, suggested the Indian by the delicacy of his perceptions and his familiarity with all that goes forward, or stands still, in wood and field. Thoreau could find his path in the woods at night, he said, better by his feet than his eyes.

"He was a good swimmer," says Emerson, "a good runner, skater, boatman, and would outwalk most countrymen in a day's journey. And the relation of body to mind was still finer. The length of his walk uniformly made the length of his writing. If shut up in the house, he did not write at all."

In his last illness says Channing, —

"His habit of engrossing his thoughts in a

journal, which had lasted for a quarter of a century, — his out-door life, of which he used to say, if he omitted that, all his living ceased, — this now became so incontrovertibly a thing of the past that he said once, standing at the window, 'I cannot see on the outside at all. We thought ourselves great philosophers in those wet days when we used to go out and sit down by the wall-sides.' This was absolutely all he was ever heard to say of that outward world during his illness, neither could a stranger in the least infer that he had ever a friend in field or wood."

This out-door life began as early as he could recollect, and his special attraction to rivers, woods, and lakes was a thing of his boyhood. He had begun to collect Indian relics before leaving college, and was a diligent student of natural history there. Whether he was naturally an observer or not (which has been denied in a kind of malicious paradox), let his life-work attest. Early in 1847 he made some collections of fishes, turtles, etc., in Concord for Agassiz, then newly arrived in America, and I have (in a letter of May 3, 1847) this account of their reception: —

"I carried them immediately to Mr. Agassiz,

who was highly delighted with them. Some of the species he had seen before, but never in so fresh condition. Others, as the breams and the pout, he had seen only in spirits, and the little turtle he knew only from the books. I am sure you would have felt fully repaid for your trouble, if you could have seen the eager satisfaction with which he surveyed each fin and scale. He said the small mud-turtle was really a very rare species, quite distinct from the snapping-turtle. The breams and pout seemed to please the Professor very much. He would gladly come up to Concord to make a spearing excursion, as you suggested, but is drawn off by numerous and pressing engagements."

On the 27th of May, Thoreau's correspondent says: —

"Mr. Agassiz was very much surprised and pleased at the extent of the collections you sent during his absence; the little fox he has established in comfortable quarters in his back-yard, where he is doing well. Among the fishes you sent there is one, probably two, new species."

June 1st, in other collections, other new species were discovered, much to Agassiz's delight, who never failed afterward to cultivate Thoreau's society when he could. But the poet avoided the man of science, having no love for dissection; though he recognized in Agassiz the qualities that gave him so much distinction.

The paper on "Ktaadn and the Maine Woods," which Horace Greeley bought "at a Jew's bargain," and sold to a publisher for seventy-five dollars, was the journal of a visit made to the highest mountain of Maine during Thoreau's second summer at Walden. An aunt of his had married in Bangor, Maine, and her daughters had again married there, so that the young forester of Concord had kinsmen on the Penobscot, engaged in converting the Maine forests into pine lumber. At the end of August, in 1846, while his Carlyle manuscript was passing from Greeley to Griswold, from Griswold to Graham, and from Graham to the Philadelphia type-setters, Thoreau himself was on his way from Boston to Bangor; and on the first day of September he started with his cousin from Bangor, to explore the upper waters of the Penobscot and climb the summit of Ktaadn. The forest region about this mountain had been explored in 1837 by Dr. Jackson, the State Geologist, a brother-in-law of Mr. Emerson; but no poet before Thoreau had visited these solitudes and described his experiences there. James Russell Lowell did so a few years later, and, early in the century, Hawthorne, Longfellow, and Emerson had tested the solitude of the Maine woods, and written about them. The verses of Emerson, describing his own experiences there (not so well known as they should be), are often thought to imply Thoreau, though they were written before Emerson had known his younger friend, whose after adventures they portray with felicity.

"In unploughed Maine he sought the lumberers' gang,
Where from a hundred lakes young rivers sprang;
He trod the unplanted forest-floor, whereon
The all-seeing sun for ages hath not shone;
Where feeds the moose and walks the surly bear,
And up the tall mast runs the woodpecker.
He saw beneath dim aisles, in odorous beds,
The slight Linnæa hang its twin-born heads,
And blessed the monument of the man of flowers,
Which breathes his sweet fame through the northern bowers.
He heard, when in the grove, at intervals
With sudden roar the aged pine-tree falls,—
One crash, the death-hymn of the perfect tree,
Declares the close of its green century.
. . . .

Through these green tents, by eldest Nature dressed,
He roamed, content alike with man and beast,
Where darkness found him he lay glad at night;
There the red morning touched him with its light.
Three moons his great heart him a hermit made,
So long he roved at will the boundless shade."

Thus much is a picture of the Maine forests, and may have been suggested in part by the woodland life of Dr. Jackson there while surveying the State. But what follows is the brave proclamation of the poet, for himself and his heroes, among whom Thoreau and John Brown must be counted, since it declares their creed and practice, — while in the last couplet the whole inner doctrine of Transcendentalism is set forth: —

"The timid it concerns to ask their way,
And fear what foes in caves and swamps can stray,
To make no step until the event is known,
And ills to come as evils past bemoan.
Not so the wise: no timid watch he keeps
To spy what danger on his pathway creeps;
Go where he will the wise man is at home,
His hearth the earth, his hall the azure dome;
Where his clear spirit leads him, there 's his road,
By God's own light illumined and foreshowed."

Thoreau may have heard these verses read by their author in his study, before he set forth on his first journey to Maine in

1838; they were first published in the "Dial" in October, 1840, but are omitted, for some reason, in the last edition of Emerson's Poems (in 1876). He never complied with this description so far as to spend three months in the Maine woods, even in the three campaigns which he made there (in 1846, in 1853, and in 1857), for in none of these did he occupy three weeks, and in all but little more than a month. His account of them, as now published, makes a volume by itself, which his friend Channing edited two years after Thoreau's death, and which contains the fullest record of his studies of the American Indian. It was his purpose to develop these studies into a book concerning the Indian, and for this purpose he made endless readings in the Jesuit Fathers, in books of travel, and in all the available literature of the subject. But the papers he had thus collected were not left in such form that they could be published; and so much of his untiring diligence seems now lost, almost thrown away. Doubtless his friend and editor, Mr. Blake, will one day print detached portions of these studies, from entries in his journals, and from his commonplace books.

In his explorations of Concord and its vicinity, as well as in those longer foot-journeys which he took among the mountains and along the sea-shore of New England, from 1838 to 1860, Thoreau's habits were those of an experienced hunter, though he seldom used a gun in his years of manhood. Upon this point he says in "Walden": —

"Almost every New England boy among my contemporaries shouldered a fowling-piece between the ages of ten and fourteen; and his hunting and fishing grounds were not limited, like the preserves of an English nobleman, but were more boundless than even those of the savage. Perhaps I have owed to fishing and hunting, when quite young, my closest acquaintance with Nature. They early introduce us to and detain us in scenery with which, otherwise, at that age, we should have little acquaintance. Fishermen, hunters, wood-choppers, and others, spending their lives in the fields and woods, in a peculiar sense a part of Nature themselves, are often in a more favorable mood for observing her, in the intervals of their pursuits, than philosophers or poets, even, who approach her with expectation. She is not afraid to exhibit herself to them. . . . I have actually fished from the same kind of necessity that the first fishers did. I have long felt differently about fowling, and sold my gun before I went to the woods. I did not pity the fishes nor the worms. As for fowling, during the last years that I carried a gun my excuse was that I was studying ornithology, and sought only new or rare birds. But I am now inclined to think there is a finer way of studying ornithology than this. It requires so much closer attention to the habits of the birds that, if for that reason only, I have been willing to omit the gun. . . . We cannot but pity the boy who has never fired a gun; he is no more humane, while his education has been sadly neglected."

Emerson mentions that Thoreau preferred his spy-glass to his gun to bring the bird nearer to his eye, and says also of his patience in out-door observation: —

"He knew how to sit immovable, a part of the rock he rested on, until the bird, the reptile, the fish, which had retired from him, should come back and resume its habits, — nay, moved by curiosity, should come to him and watch him."

And I have thought that Emerson had

Thoreau in mind when he described his "Forester": —

"He took the color of his vest
From rabbit's coat or grouse's breast;
For as the wood-kinds lurk and hide,
So walks the woodman unespied."

The same friend said of him: —

"It was a pleasure and a privilege to walk with him. He knew the country like a fox or bird, and passed through it as freely by paths of his own. Under his arm he carried an old music-book to press plants;[1] in his pocket his diary and pencil, a spy-glass for birds, microscope, jack-knife, and twine. He wore straw hat, stout shoes, strong gray trousers, to brave shrub-oaks and smilax, and to climb a tree for a hawk's or squirrel's nest. He waded into the pool for the water-plants, and his strong legs were no insignificant part of his armor. His intimacy with animals suggested what Thomas Fuller records of Butler the apiologist, 'that either he had told the bees things, or the bees had told him.' Snakes coiled round his leg, the fishes swam into his hand, and he took them out of the water; he

[1] It was a "Primo Flauto" of his father's, who, like himself, was a sweet player on the flute, and had performed with that instrument in the parish choir, before the day of church-organs in Concord.

pulled the woodchuck out of its hole by the tail, and took the foxes under his protection from the hunters. He confessed that he sometimes felt like a hound or a panther, and, if born among Indians, would have been a fell hunter. But, restrained by his Massachusetts culture, he played out the game in the mild form of botany and ichthyology. His power of observation seemed to indicate additional senses; he saw as with microscope, heard as with ear-trumpet, and his memory was a photographic register of all he saw and heard. Every fact lay in order and glory in his mind, a type of the order and beauty of the whole."

It was this poetic and coördinating vision of the natural world which distinguished Thoreau from the swarm of naturalists, and raised him to the rank of a philosopher even in his tedious daily observations. Channing, no less than Emerson, has observed and noted this trait, giving to his friend the exact title of "poet-naturalist," and also, in his poem, "The Wanderer," bestowing on him the queer name of *Idolon*, which he thus explains: —

"So strangely was the general current mixed
With his vexed native blood in its crank wit,
That as a mirror shone the common world

To this observing youth, — whom noting, thence
I called *Idolon*, — ever firm to mark
Swiftly reflected in himself the Whole."

In an earlier poem Channing had called him "Rudolpho," and had thus portrayed his daily and nightly habits of observation: —

"I see Rudolpho cross our honest fields
Collapsed with thought, and as the Stagyrite
At intellectual problems, mastering
Day after day part of the world's concern.
Nor welcome dawns nor shrinking nights him menace,
Still adding to his list beetle and bee, —
Of what the vireo builds a pensile nest,
And why the peetweet drops her giant egg
In wheezing meadows, odorous with sweet brake.
Who wonders that the flesh declines to grow
Along his sallow pits? or that his life,
To social pleasure careless, pines away
In dry seclusion and unfruitful shade?
I must admire thy brave apprenticeship
To those dry forages, although the worldling
Laugh in his sleeve at thy compelled devotion.
So shalt thou learn, Rudolpho, as thou walk'st,
More from the winding lanes where Nature leaves
Her unaspiring creatures, and surpass
In some fine saunter her acclivity."

The hint here given that Thoreau injured his once robust health by his habits of outdoor study and the hardships he imposed on himself, had too much truth in it. Growing up with great strength of body and limb, and having cultivated his physical advantages by a temperate youth much exercised with manual labor, in which he took pleasure, Thoreau could not learn the lesson of moderation in those pursuits to which his nature inclined. He exposed himself in his journeys and night encampments to cold and hunger, and changes of weather, which the strongest cannot brave with impunity. Mr. Edward Hoar, who traveled with him in the Maine woods in 1857, — a journey of three hundred and twenty-five miles with a canoe and an Indian, among the head-waters of the Kennebec, Penobscot, and St. John's rivers, — and who in 1858 visited the White Mountains with him, remembers, with a shiver to this day, the rigor of a night spent on the bare rocks of Mount Washington, with insufficient blankets, — Thoreau sleeping from habit, but himself lying wakeful all night, and gazing at the coldest of full moons. It was after such an experience as this on Monadnoc, whither Thoreau and Channing went to camp out for a week in August, 1860, that the latter wrote: —

"With the night,
Reserved companion, cool and sparsely clad,
Dream, till the threefold hour with lowly voice
Steals whispering in thy frame, 'Rise, valiant youth!
The dawn draws on apace, envious of thee,
And polar in his gait; advance thy limbs,
Nor strive to heat the stones.'"

Thoreau had much scorn for weakness like this, and said of his comrade, "I fear that he did not improve all the night as he might have done, to sleep." This was his last excursion, and he died within less than two years afterward. The account of it which Channing has given may therefore be read with interest: —

"He ascended such hills as Monadnoc by his own path; would lay down his map on the summit and draw a line to the point he proposed to visit below, — perhaps forty miles away on the landscape, and set off bravely to make the 'short-cut.' The lowland people wondered to see him scaling the heights as if he had lost his way, or at his jumping over their cow-yard fences, — asking if he had fallen from the clouds. In a walk like this he always carried his umbrella; and on this Monadnoc trip, when about a mile from the station (in Troy, N. H.), a torrent of rain came down; without the umbrella his books, blankets, maps, and provisions would all have been spoiled, or the morning lost by delay. On the mountain there being a thick soaking fog, the first object was to camp and make tea.[1] He spent five nights in camp, having built another hut, to get varied views. Flowers, birds, lichens, and the rocks were carefully examined, all parts of the mountain were visited, and as accurate a map as could be made by pocket compass was carefully sketched and drawn out, in the five days spent there, — with notes of the striking aerial phenomena, incidents of travel and natural history. The fatigue, the blazing sun, the face getting broiled, the pint-cup never scoured, shaving unutterable, your stockings dreary, having taken to peat, — not all the books in the world, as Sancho says, could contain the adventures of a week in camping. The wild, free life, the open air, the new and strange sounds by night and day, the odd and bewildering rocks, amid which a person can be lost within a rod of camp; the strange cries of visitors to the summit; the great

[1] Thoreau says of this adventure: "After putting our packs under a rock, having a good hatchet, I proceeded to build a substantial house. This was done about dark, and by that time we were as wet as if we had stood in a hogshead of water. We then built a fire before the door, directly on the site of our camp of two years ago. Standing before this, and turning round slowly, like meat that is roasting, we were as dry, if not drier than ever, after a few hours, and so, at last, we turned in."

valley over to Wachusett, with its thunder-storms and battles in the cloud; the farmers' back-yards in Jaffrey, where the family cotton can be seen bleaching on the grass, but no trace of the pigmy family; the dry, soft air all night, the lack of dew in the morning; the want of water, — a pint being a good deal, — these, and similar things make up some part of such an excursion."

These excursions were common with Thoreau, but less so with Channing, who therefore, notes down many things that his friend would not think worth recording, except as a part of that calendar of Nature which he set himself to keep, and of which his journals, for more than twenty years, are the record. From these he made up his printed volumes, and there may be read the details that he registered. He had gauges for the height of the river, noted the temperature of springs and ponds, the tints of the morning and evening sky, the flowering and fruit of plants, all the habits of birds and animals, and every aspect of nature from the smallest to the greatest. Much of this is the dryest detail, but everywhere you come upon strokes of beauty, in a single word-picture, or in a page of idyllic description, like this of the Concord heifer, which might be a poem of Theocritus, or one of the lost bucolics of Moschus: —

"One more confiding heifer, the fairest of the herd, did by degrees approach, as if to take some morsel from our hands, while our hearts leaped to our mouths with expectation and delight. She by degrees drew near with her fair limbs progressive, making pretense of browsing; nearer and nearer till there was wafted to us the bovine fragrance, — cream of all the dairies that ever were or will be, — and then she raised her gentle muzzle toward us, and snuffed an honest recognition within hand's reach. I saw it was possible for his herd to inspire with love the herdsman. She was as delicately featured as a hind; her hide was mingled white and fawn color; on her muzzle's tip there was a white spot not bigger than a daisy; and on her side turned toward me the map of Asia plain to see. Farewell, dear heifer! though thou forgettest me, my prayer to heaven shall be that thou may'st not forget thyself.

"I saw her name was Sumach. And by the kindred spots I knew her mother, more sedate and matronly, with full-grown bag, and on her sides was Asia, great and small, the plains of Tartary, even to the pole, while on her daughter's was Asia Minor. She was not disposed to wanton with the herdsman. As I walked the heifer followed me, and took an apple from my hand, and seemed to care more for the hand than the apple. So innocent a face I have rarely seen on any creature, and I have looked in the face of many heifers; and as she took the apple from my hand, I caught the apple of her eye. There was no sinister expression. She smelled as sweet as the clethra blossom. For horns, though she had them, they were so well disposed in the right place, but neither up nor down, that I do not now remember she had any."

Or take this apostrophe to the "Queen of Night, the Huntress Diana," which is not a translation from some Greek worshipper, but the sincere ascription of a New England hunter of the noblest deer:—

"My dear, my dewy sister, let thy rain descend on me! I not only love thee, but I love the best of thee, — that is to love thee rarely. I do not love thee every day — commonly I love those who are less than thee; I love thee only on great days. Thy dewy words feed me like the manna of the morning. I am as much thy sister as thy brother; thou art as much my brother as my sister. It is a portion of thee and a portion of me which are of kin. O my sister! O Diana! thy tracks are on the eastern hill; thou newly didst pass that way. I, the hunter, saw them in the morning dew. My eyes are the hounds that pursued thee. I hear thee; thou canst speak, I cannot; I fear and forget to answer; I am occupied with hearing. I awoke and thought of thee; thou wast present to my mind. How camest thou there? Was I not present to thee, likewise?"

In such a lofty mystical strain did this Concord Endymion declare his passion for Nature, in whose green lap he slumbers now on the hill-side which the goddess nightly revisits.

"O sister of the sun, draw near,
With softly-moving step and slow,
For dreaming not of earthly woe
Thou seest Endymion sleeping here!"

CHAPTER XI.

PERSONAL TRAITS AND SOCIAL LIFE.

THE face of Thoreau, once seen, could not easily be forgotten, so strong was the mark that genius had set upon it. The portrait of him, which has been commonly engraved, though it bore some resemblance at the time it was taken (by S. W. Rowse, in 1854), was never a very exact likeness. A few years later he began to wear his beard long, and this fine silken muffler for his delicate throat and lungs, was also an ornament to his grave and thoughtful face, concealing its weakest feature, a receding chin. The head engraved for this volume is from a photograph taken, in 1861, at New Bedford, and shows him as he was in his last years. His personal traits were not startling and commanding like, those of Webster, who drew the eyes of all men wherever he appeared, but they were peculiar, and dwelt long in the memory. His features were prominent, his eyes large, round, and deep-set, under bold brows, and full of fearless meditation; the color varying from blue to gray, as if with the moods of his mind. A youth who saw him for the first time, said with a start, "How deep and clear is the mark that *thought* sets upon a man's face!" And, indeed, no man could fail to recognize in him that rare intangible essence we call *thought;* his slight figure was active with it, while in his face it became contemplative, as if, like his own peasant, he were "meditating some vast and sunny problem." Channing says of his appearance:—

"In height he was about the average; in his build spare, with limbs that were rather longer than usual, or of which he made a longer use. His features were marked; the nose aquiline or very Roman, like one of the portraits of Cæsar (more like a beak, as was said); large overhanging brows above the deepest-set blue eyes that could be seen, — blue in certain lights and in others gray; the forehead not unusually broad or high, full of concentrated energy and purpose; the mouth with prominent lips, pursed up with meaning and thought when silent, and giving out when open a stream of the most varied and unusual and instructive sayings. His whole figure had an active earnestness, as if he had no moment to waste; the clenched hand betokened purpose. In walking he made a short cut, if he could, and when sitting in the shade or by the wall-side, seemed merely the clearer to look forward into the next piece of activity. The intensity of his mind, like Dante's, conveyed the breathing of aloofness, — his eyes bent on the ground, his long swinging gait, his hands perhaps clasped behind him, or held closely at his side, — the fingers made into a fist."

It is not possible to describe him more exactly.

In December, 1854, Thoreau went to lecture at Nantucket, and on his way spent a day or two with one of his correspondents, Daniel Ricketson of New Bedford, — reaching his house on Christmas day. His host, who then saw him for the first time, thus recorded his impressions: —

"I had expected him at noon, but as he did not arrive, I had given him up for the day. In the latter part of the afternoon, I was clearing off the snow, which had fallen during the day, from my front steps, when, looking up, I saw a man walking up the carriage-road, bearing a portmanteau in one hand and an umbrella in the other. He was dressed in a long overcoat of dark color, and wore a dark soft hat. I had no suspicion it was Thoreau, and rather supposed it was a pedler of small wares."

This was a common mistake to make about Thoreau. When he ran the gauntlet of the Cape Cod villages, — "feeling as strange," he says, "as if he were in a town in China," — one of the old fishermen could not believe that he had not something to sell, as Bronson Alcott had when he perambulated Eastern Virginia and North Carolina in 1819–22, peddling silks and jewelry. Being assured that Thoreau was not peddling spectacles or books, the fisherman said at last: "Well, it makes no odds what it is you carry, so long as you carry Truth along with you."

"As Thoreau came near me," continues Mr. Ricketson, "he stopped and said, 'You do not know me.' It flashed at once on my mind that the person before me was my correspondent, whom in my imagination I had figured as stout and robust, instead of the small and rather inferior-looking man before me. I concealed my disappointment, and at once replied, 'I presume this is Mr. Thoreau.' Taking his portmanteau,

I conducted him to his room, already awaiting him. My disappointment at his personal appearance passed off on hearing his conversation at the table and during the evening; and rarely through the years of my acquaintance with him did his presence conflict with his noble powers of mind, his rich conversation, and broad erudition. His face was afterwards greatly improved in manly expression by the growth of his beard, which he wore in full during the later years of his life; but when I first saw him he had just been sitting for the crayon portrait of 1854, which represents him without the beard. The 'ambrotype' of him, which is engraved for your volume, was taken for me by Dunshee, at New Bedford, August 21, 1861, on his last visit to me at Brooklawn. His health was then failing, — he had a racking cough, — but his face, except a shade of sadness in the eyes, did not show it. Of this portrait, Miss Sophia Thoreau, to whom I sent it soon after her brother's death, wrote me, May 26, 1862: 'I cannot tell you how agreeably surprised I was, on opening the little box, to find my own lost brother again. I could not restrain my tears. The picture is invaluable to us. I discover a slight shade about the eyes, expressive of weariness; but a stranger might not observe it. I am very glad to possess a picture of so late a date. The crayon, drawn eight years ago next summer, we considered good; it betrays the poet. Mr. Channing, Mr. Emerson, Mr. Alcott, and many other friends who have looked at the ambrotype, express much satisfaction.' "

Of Thoreau's appearance then (at the age of thirty-seven), Mr. Ricketson goes on to say: —

"The most expressive feature of his face was his eye, blue in color, and full of the greatest humanity and intelligence. His head was of medium size, the same as that of Emerson, and he wore a number seven hat. His arms were rather long, his legs short, and his hands and feet rather large. His sloping shoulders were a mark of observation. But when in usual health he was strong and vigorous, a remarkable pedestrian, tiring out nearly all his companions in his prolonged tramps through woods and marshes, when in pursuit of some rare plant. In Thoreau, as in Dr. Kane, Lord Nelson, and other heroic men, it was the spirit more than the temple in which it dwelt, that made the man."

A strange mistake has prevailed as to the supposed churlishness and cynical severity of Thoreau, which Mr. Alcott, in one of his octogenarian sonnets, has corrected, and which all who knew the man would protest against.

Of his domestic character Mr. Ricketson writes: —

"Some have accused him of being an imitator of Emerson, others as unsocial, impracticable, and ascetic. Now, he was none of these. A more original man never lived, nor one more thoroughly a personification of civility. Having been an occasional guest at his house, I can assert that no man could hold a finer relationship with his family than he."

Channing says the same thing more quaintly: —

"In his own home he was one of those characters who may be called household treasures; always on the spot with skillful eye and hand, to raise the best melons, plant the orchard with the choicest trees, and act as extempore mechanic; fond of the pets, — his sister's flowers or sacred tabby — kittens being his favorites, — he would play with them by the half hour."

He was sometimes given to music and song, and now and then, in moments of great hilarity, would dance gayly, — as he did once at Brooklawn, in the presence of his host, Mr. Ricketson, and Mr. Alcott, who was also visiting there. On the same occasion he sung his unique song of "Tom Bowline," which none who heard would ever forget, and finished the evening with his dance.

Hearing Mr. Ricketson speak of this dance, Miss Thoreau said: —

"I have so often witnessed the like, that I can easily imagine how it was; and I remember that Henry gave me some account of it. I recollect he said he did not scruple to tread on Mr. Alcott's toes."

Mr. Ricketson's own account is this: —

"One afternoon, when my wife was playing an air upon the piano, — 'Highland Laddie,' perhaps, — Thoreau became very hilarious, sang 'Tom Bowline,' and finally entered upon an improvised dance. Not being able to stand what appeared to me at the time the somewhat ludicrous appearance of our Walden hermit, I retreated to my 'shanty,' a short distance from my house; while my older and more humor-loving friend Alcott remained and saw it through, much to his amusement. It left a pleasant memory, which I recorded in some humble lines that afterwards appeared in my 'Autumn Sheaf.'"

After Thoreau's return home from this

visit, his New Bedford friend seems to have sent him a copy of the words and music of "Tom Bowline," which was duly acknowledged and handed over to the musical people of Concord for them to play and sing. It is a fine old pathetic sailor-song of Dibdin's, which pleased Thoreau (whose imagination delighted in the sea), and perhaps reminded him of his brother John. As Thoreau sang it, the verses ran thus: —

"Here a sheer hulk lies poor Tom Bowline,
The darling of our crew;
No more he 'll hear the tempest howling,
For death has broached him to.
His form was of the manliest beauty;
His heart was kind and soft;
Faithful, below, he did his duty,
But now he 's gone aloft.

"Tom never from his word departed,
His virtues were so rare;
His friends were many and true-hearted,
His Poll was kind and fair.
And then he 'd sing so blithe and jolly;
Ah, many 's the time and oft!
But mirth is changed to melancholy,
For Tom is gone aloft.

"Yet shall poor Tom find pleasant weather
When He who all commands
Shall give, to call life's crew together,
The word to pipe all hands.

Thus death, who kings and tars dispatches,
In vain Tom's life has doffed;
For though his body 's under hatches,
His soul is gone aloft!"

Another of his songs was Moore's "Canadian Boat Song," with its chorus, —

"Row brothers, row."

A lady who knew him when she was a child, from the age of six to that of fifteen more particularly, and who first remembers him in his hut at Walden, writes me: —

"The time when Mr. Thoreau was our more intimate playfellow must have been in the years from 1850 to 1855. He used to come in, at dusk, as my brother and I sat on the rug before the dining-room fire, and, taking the great green rocking-chair, he would tell us stories. Those I remember were his own adventures, as a child. He began with telling us of the different houses he had lived in, and what he could remember about each. The house where he was born was on the Virginia road, near the old Bedford road. The only thing he remembered about that house was that from its windows he saw a flock of geese walking along in a row on the other side of the road; but to show what a long memory he had, when he told his mother of this, she said the only time he could have seen that sight was, when he was about eight months old, for they left that house then. Soon after, he lived in the old house on the Lexington road, nearly opposite Mr. Emerson's. There he was tossed by a cow as he played near the door, in his red flannel dress,— and so on, with a story for every house. He used to delight us with the adventures of a brood of fall chickens, which slept at night in a tall old fashioned fig-drum in the kitchen, and as their bed was not changed when they grew larger, they packed themselves every night each in its own place, and grew up, not shapely, but shaped to each other and the drum, like figs!

"Sometimes he would play juggler tricks for us, and swallow his knife and produce it again from our ears or noses. We usually ran to bring some apples for him as soon as he came in, and often he would cut one in halves in fine points that scarcely showed on close examination, and then the joke was to ask Father to break it for us and see it fall to pieces in his hands. But perhaps the evenings most charming were those when he brought some ears of pop-corn in his pocket and headed an expedition to the garret to hunt out the old brass warming-pan; in which he would put the corn, and hold it out and shake it over the fire till it was heated through, and at last, as we listened, the rattling changed to popping. When this became very brisk, he would hold the pan over the rug and lift the lid, and a beautiful fountain of the white corn flew all over us. It required both strength and patience to hold out the heavy warming-pan at arm's length so long, and no one else ever gave us that pleasure.

"I remember his singing 'Tom Bowline' to us, and also playing on his flute, but that was earlier. In the summer he used to make willow whistles, and trumpets out of the stems of squash leaves, and onion leaves. When he found fine berries during his walks, he always remembered us, and came to arrange a huckleberrying for us. He took charge of the 'hay rigging' with the load of children, who sat on the floor which was spread with hay, covered with a buffalo-robe; he sat on a board placed across the front and drove, and led the frolic with his jokes and laughter as we jolted along, while the elders of the family accompanied us in a 'carryall.' Either he had great tact and skill in managing us and keeping our spirits and play within bounds, or else he became a child in sympathy with us, for I do not remember a check or reproof from him, no matter how noisy we were. He always was most kind to me and made it his especial care to establish me in the 'thickest places,' as we used to call them. Those sunny afternoons are bright memories, and the lamb-kill flowers and sweet 'everlasting,' always recall them and his kind care. Once in awhile he took us on the river in his boat, a rare pleasure then; and I remember one brilliant autumn afternoon, when he took us to gather the wild grapes overhanging the river, and we brought home a load of crimson and golden boughs as well. He never took us to walk with him, but sometimes joined us for a little way, if he met us in the woods on Sunday afternoons. He made those few steps memorable by showing us many wonders in so short a space: perhaps the only chincapin oak in Concord, so hidden that no one but himself could have discovered it — or some remarkable bird, or nest, or flower. He took great interest in my garden of wild flowers, and used to bring me seeds, or roots, of rare plants. In his last illness it did not occur to us that he would care to see us, but his sister told my mother that he watched us from the window as we passed, and said: 'Why don't they come to see me? I love them as if they were my own.' After that we went often, and he always made us so welcome that we liked to go. I remember our last meetings with as much pleasure as the old play-days."

Although so great a traveler in a small circle — being every day a-field when not too ill, — he was also a great stay-at-home.

He never crossed the ocean, nor saw Niagara or the Mississippi until the year before his death. He lived within twenty miles of Boston, but seldom went there, except to pass through it on his way to the Maine woods, to Cape Cod, to the house of his friend, Marston Watson at Plymouth, or to Daniel Ricketson's at New Bedford. To the latter he wrote in February, 1855: —

"I did not go to Boston, for, with regard to that place I sympathize with one of my neighbors (George Minott), an old man, who has not been there since the last war, when he was compelled to go. No, I have a real genius for staying at home."

What took him from home in the winter season was generally some engagement to lecture, of which he had many after his Walden life became a little known abroad.

From the year 1847 Thoreau may be said to have fairly entered on his career as author and lecturer; having taken all the needful degrees and endured most of the mortifications necessary for the public profession of authorship. Up to that time he had supported himself, except while in college, chiefly by the labor of his hands;

after 1847, though still devoted to manual labor occasionally, he yet worked chiefly with his head as thinker, observer, surveyor, magazine contributor, and lecturer.

His friends were the first promoters of his lectures, and among his correspondence are some letters from Hawthorne, inviting him to the Salem Lyceum. The first of these letters is dated, Salem, October 21, 1848, and runs thus: —

"My dear Sir, — The managers of the Salem Lyceum, sometime ago, voted that you should be requested to deliver a lecture before that Institution during the approaching season. I know not whether Mr. Chever, the late corresponding secretary, communicated the vote to you; at all events, no answer has been received, and as Mr. Chever's successor in office, I am requested to repeat the invitation. Permit me to add my own earnest wishes that you will accept it; and also, laying aside my official dignity, to express my wife's desire and my own that you will be our guest, if you do come. In case of your compliance, the Managers desire to know at what time it will best suit you to deliver the lecture. Very truly yours,

"Nath[l] Hawthorne,

"*Cor. Sec'y, Salem Lyceum.*

"P. S. I live at No. 14 Mall Street, where I shall be very happy to see you. The stated fee for lectures is $20."

A month later, Hawthorne, who had received an affirmative answer from Thoreau, wrote to him from Boston (November 20, 1848), as follows: —

"MY DEAR THOREAU, — I did not sooner write you, because there were preëngagements for the two or three first lectures, so that I could not arrange matters to have you come during the present month. But, as it happens, the expected lectures have failed us, and we now depend on you to come the very next Wednesday. I shall announce you in the paper of to-morrow, so you *must* come. I regret that I could not give you longer notice. We shall expect you on Wednesday at No. 14 Mall Street. Yours truly,

"NATH[L] HAWTHORNE.

"If it be utterly impossible for you to come, pray write me a line so that I may get it Wednesday evening. But by all means come.

"This secretaryship is an intolerable bore. I have traveled thirty miles, this wet day, on no other business."

Apparently another lecture was wanted by the Salem people the same winter, for on the 19th of February, 1849, when the "Week on the Concord and Merrimac" was in press, Hawthorne wrote again, thus: —

"The managers request that you will lecture before the Salem Lyceum on Wednesday evening *after* next, that is to say, on the 28th inst. May we depend on you? Please to answer immediately, if convenient. Mr. Alcott delighted my wife and me, the other evening, by announcing that you had a book in press. I rejoice at it, and nothing doubt of such success as will be worth having. Should your manuscripts all be in the printer's hands, I suppose you can reclaim one of them for a single evening's use, to be returned the next morning, — or perhaps that Indian lecture, which you mentioned to me, is in a state of forwardness. Either that, or a continuation of the Walden experiment (or indeed, anything else), will be acceptable. We shall expect you at 14 Mall Street. Very truly yours,

"NATH[L] HAWTHORNE."

These letters were written just before Hawthorne was turned out of his office in the Salem custom-house, and while his own literary success was still in abeyance, — the "Scarlet Letter" not being published till a year later. They show the friendly terms on which Hawthorne stood with the Concord Transcendentalists, after leaving that town in 1846. He returned to it in 1852, when he bought Mr. Alcott's estate, then called "Hillside," which he afterward christened "Wayside," and by this name it is still known. Mr. Alcott bought this place in 1845, and from then till 1848, when he left it to reside in Boston, he expended, as Hawthorne said, "a good deal of taste and some money in forming the hill-side behind the house into terraces, and building arbors and summer-houses of rough stems, and branches, and trees, on a system of his own." In this work he was aided by Thoreau, who was then in the habit of performing much manual labor. In 1847 he joined Mr. Alcott in the task of cutting trees for Mr. Emerson's summer-house, which the three friends were to build in the garden. Mr. Emerson, however, went with them to the woods but one day, when finding his strength and skill unequal to that of his companions, he withdrew, and left the work to them. Mr. Alcott relates that Thoreau was not only a master workman with the axe, but also had such strength of arm, that when a tree they were felling lodged in some unlucky position, he rushed at it, and by main strength carried out the trunk until it fell where he wanted it.

It was one of the serious doctrines of the Transcendentalists that each person should perform his quota of hand-work, and accordingly Alcott, Channing, Hawthorne, and the rest, took their turn at wood-chopping, hay-making, plowing, tree-pruning, grafting, etc. Even Emerson trimmed his own orchard, and sometimes lent a hand in hoeing corn and raking hay. To Thoreau such tasks were easy, and, unlike some amateur farmers, he was quite willing to be seen at his work, whatever it might be (except the pencil-making, in which there were certain secrets), and by choice he wore plain working clothes, and generally old ones. The fashion of his garments gave him no concern, and was often old, or even grotesque. At one time he had a fancy for corduroy, such as Irish laborers then wore, but which occasionally appeared in the wardrobe of a gentleman. As he climbed trees, waded swamps, and was out in all weathers during his daily excursions, he naturally dressed himself for what he had to do.

As may be inferred from his correspondence with Horace Greeley, Thoreau's whole income from authorship during the twenty years that he practiced that profession, cannot have exceeded a few hundred dollars yearly, — not half enough in most years to supply even his few wants. He would never be indebted to any person pecuniarily, and therefore he found out other ways of earning his subsistence and paying his obligations, — gardening, fence-building, white-washing, pencil-making, land-surveying, etc., — for he had great mechanical skill, and a patient, conscientious industry in whatever he undertook. When his father, who had been long living in other men's houses, undertook, at last, to build one of his own, Henry worked upon it, and performed no small part of the manual labor. He had no false pride in such matters, — was, indeed, rather proud of his workmanship, and averse to the gentility even of his industrious village.

During his first residence at Mr. Emerson's in 1841–43, Thoreau managed the garden and did other hand-work for his friend; and when Mr. Emerson went to England in 1847, he returned to the house (soon after leaving his Walden hut), and took charge of his friend's household affairs in his absence. In a letter to his sister Sophia (October 24, 1847), Thoreau says:—

". . . I went to Boston the 5th of this month to see Mr. Emerson off to Europe. He sailed in the 'Washington Irving' packet ship, the same in which Mr. Hedge went before him. Up to this trip, the first mate aboard this ship was, as I hear, one Stephens, a Concord boy, son of Stephens, the carpenter, who used to live above Mr. Dennis. Mr. Emerson's state-room was like a carpeted dark closet, about six feet square, with a large keyhole for a window (the window was about as big as a saucer, and the glass two inches thick), not to mention another skylight overhead in the deck, of the size of an oblong doughnut, and about as opaque. Of course, it would be in vain to look up, if any contemplative promenader put his foot upon it. Such will be his lodgings for two or three weeks; and instead of a walk in Walden woods, he will take a promenade on deck, where the few trees, you know, are stripped of their bark."

There is a poem of Thoreau's, of uncertain date, called "The Departure," which, as I suppose, expresses his emotions at leaving finally, in 1848, the friendly house of Emerson, where he had dwelt so long, upon terms of such ideal intimacy. It was never seen by his friends, so far as I can learn, until after his death, when Sophia Thoreau gave it to me, along with other poems, for publication in the "Boston Commonwealth," in 1863. Since then it has been mentioned as a poem written in anticipation of death. This is not so; it was certainly written long before his illness.

"In this roadstead I have ridden,
In this covert I have hidden:
Friendly thoughts were cliffs to me,
And I hid beneath their lea.

"This true people took the stranger,
And warm-hearted housed the ranger;
They received their roving guest,
And have fed him with the best;

"Whatsoe'er the land afforded
To the stranger's wish accorded,—
Shook the olive, stripped the vine,
And expressed the strengthening wine.

"And by night they did spread o'er him
What by day they spread before him;

That good will which was repast
Was his covering at last.

"The stranger moored him to their pier
Without anxiety or fear;
By day he walked the sloping land,—
By night the gentle heavens he scanned.

"When first his bark stood inland
To the coast of that far Finland,
Sweet-watered brooks came tumbling to the shore,
The weary mariner to restore.

"And still he stayed from day to day,
If he their kindness might repay;
But more and more
The sullen waves came rolling toward the shore.

"And still, the more the stranger waited,
The less his argosy was freighted;
And still the more he stayed,
The less his debt was paid.

"So he unfurled his shrouded mast
To receive the fragrant blast,—
And that same refreshing gale
Which had woo'd him to remain
Again and again;—
It was that filled his sail
And drove him to the main.

"All day the low hung clouds
Dropped tears into the sea,
And the wind amid the shrouds
Sighed plaintively."

CHAPTER XII.

POET, MORALIST, AND PHILOSOPHER.

THE character of poet is so high and so rare, in any modern civilization, and specially in our American career of nationality, that it behooves us to mark and claim all our true poets, before they are classified under some other name, — as philosophers, naturalists, romancers, or historians. Thus Emerson is primarily and chiefly a poet, and only a philosopher in his second intention; and thus also Thoreau, though a naturalist by habit, and a moralist by constitution, was inwardly a poet by force of that shaping and controlling imagination, which was his strongest faculty. His mind tended naturally to the ideal side. He would have been an idealist in any circumstances; a fluent and glowing poet, had he been born among a people to whom poesy is native, like the Greeks, the Italians, the Irish. As it was, his poetic light illumined every wide prospect and every narrow cranny in which his active, patient spirit pursued its task. It was this inward illumination as well as the star-like beam of Emerson's genius in "Nature," which caused Thoreau to write in his senior year at college, "This curious world which we inhabit is more wonderful than it is convenient; more beautiful than it is useful," and he cherished this belief through life. In youth, too, he said, "The other world is all my art, my pencils will draw no other, my jack-knife will cut nothing else; I do not use it as a means." It was in this spirit that he afterwards uttered the quaint parable, which was his version of the primitive legend of the Golden Age:—

"I long ago lost a hound, a bay horse, and a turtle-dove, and am still on their trail. Many are the travelers I have spoken concerning them, describing their tracks and what calls they answered to. I have met one or two who had heard the hound, and the tramp of the horse, and even seen the dove disappear behind the cloud; and they seemed as anxious to recover them as if they had lost them themselves."

In the same significance read his little-known verses, "The Pilgrims."

"When I have slumbered
I have heard sounds
As of travelers passing
These my grounds.

"'T was a sweet music
Wafted them by,
I could not tell
If afar off or nigh.

"Unless I dreamed it
This was of yore;
I never told it
To mortal before.

"Never remembered
But in my dreams,
What to me waking
A miracle seems."

It seems to have been the habit of Thoreau, in writing verse, to compose a couplet, a quatrain, or other short metrical expression, copy it in his journal, and afterward, when these verses had grown to a considerable number, to arrange them in the form of a single piece. This gives to his poems the epigrammatic air which most of them have. After he was thirty years old, he wrote scarcely any verse, and he even destroyed much that he had previously written, following in this the judgment of Mr.

Emerson, rather than his own, as he told me one day during his last illness. He had read all that was best in English and in Greek poetry, but was more familiar with the English poets of Milton's time and earlier, than with those more recent, except his own townsmen and companions. He valued Milton above Shakespeare, and had a special love for Æschylus, two of whose tragedies he translated. He had read Pindar, Simonides, and the Greek Anthology, and wrote, at his best, as well as the finest of the Greek lyric poets. Even Emerson, who was a severe critic of his verses, says, "His classic poem on 'Smoke' suggests Simonides, but is better than any poem of Simonides." Indeed, what Greek would not be proud to claim this fragment as his own?

"Light winged smoke, Icarian bird!
Melting thy pinions in thy upward flight,
Lark without song, and messenger of dawn,—
. . . .
Go thou, my incense, upward from this hearth,
And ask the gods to pardon this clear flame."

No complete collection of Thoreau's poems has ever been made. Amid much that is harsh and crude, such a book would contain many verses sure to survive for centuries.

As a moralist, the bent of Thoreau is more clearly seen by most readers; and on this side, too, he was early and strongly charged. In a college essay of 1837 are these sentences: —

"Truth neither exalteth nor humbleth herself. She is not too high for the low, nor yet too low for the high. She is persuasive, not litigious, leaving conscience to decide. She never sacrificeth her dignity that she may secure for herself a favorable reception. It is not a characteristic of Truth to use men tenderly; nor is she over-anxious about appearances."

In another essay of the same year he wrote: —

"The order of things should be reversed: the seventh should be man's day of toil, in which to earn his living by the sweat of his brow, and the other six his Sabbath of the affections and the soul, in which to range this wide-spread garden, and drink in the soft influences and sublime revelations of Nature."

This was an anticipation of his theory of labor and leisure set forth in "Walden," where he says: —

"For more than five years I maintained myself solely by the labor of my hands, and I found that, by working about six weeks in a year, I could meet all the expenses of living; the whole of my winters, as well as most of my summers, I had free and clear for study. I found that the occupation of day-laborer was the most independent of any, especially as it required only thirty or forty days in the year to support one."

This was true of Thoreau, because, as he said, his "greatest skill had been to want but little." In him this economy was a part of morality, or even of religion.

"The high moral impulse," says Channing, "never deserted him, and he resolved early to read no book, take no walk, undertake no enterprise, but such as he could endure to give an account of to himself." How early this austerity appeared in what he wrote, has been little noticed; but I discover it in his earliest college essays, before he was eighteen years old. Thus, in such a paper of the year 1834, this passage occurs: —

"There appears to be something noble, something exalted, in giving up one's own interest for that of his fellow-beings. He is a true patriot, who, casting aside all selfish thoughts, and not suffering his benevolent intentions to be polluted by thinking of the fame he is acquiring, presses forward in the great work he has undertaken, with unremitted zeal; who is as one pursuing his way through a garden abounding with fruits of every description, without turning aside, or regarding the brambles which impede his progress, but pressing onward with his eyes fixed upon the golden fruit before him. He is worthy of all praise; his is, indeed, true greatness."

In contrast with this man the young philosopher sets before us the man who wishes, as the Greeks said, πλεονεκτεῖν, — to get more than his square meal at the banquet of life.

"Aristocrats may say what they please, — liberty and equal rights are and ever will be grateful, till nature herself shall change; and he who is ambitious to exercise authority over his fellow-beings, with no view to their benefit or injury, is to be regarded as actuated by peculiarly selfish motives. Self-gratification must be his sole object. Perhaps he is desirous that his name may be handed down to posterity; that in after ages something more may be said of him than that he lived and died. His deeds may never be forgotten; but is this greatness? If so, may I pass through life unheeded and unknown!"

What was his own ambition — a purpose

in life which only the unthinking could ever confound with selfishness — was expressed by him early in a prayer which he threw into this verse: —

"Great God! I ask Thee for no meaner pelf,
Than that I may not disappoint myself;
That in my conduct I may soar as high
As I can now discern with this clear eye.
That my weak hand may equal my firm faith,
And my life practice more than my tongue saith;
That my low conduct may not show,
Nor my relenting lines,
That I thy purpose did not know,
Or overrated thy designs."

And it may be said of him that he acted this prayer as well as uttered it. Says Channing again: —

"In our estimate of his character, the moral qualities form the basis; for himself rigidly enjoined; if in another, he could overlook delinquency. Truth before all things; in all your thoughts, your faintest breath, the austerest purity, the utmost fulfilling of the interior law; faith in friends, and an iron and flinty pursuit of right, which nothing can tease or purchase out of us."

Thus it is said that when he went to prison rather than pay his tax, which went to support slavery in South Carolina, and his friend Emerson came to the cell and said, "Henry, why are you here?" the reply was, "Why are you *not* here?"

In this act, which even his best friends at first denounced as "mean and sneaking and in bad taste," — this refusal to pay the trifling sum demanded of him by the Concord tax-gatherer, — the outlines of his political philosophy appear. They were illuminated afterwards by his trenchant utterances in denunciation of slavery and in encomium of John Brown, who attacked that monster in its most vulnerable part. It was not mere whim, but a settled theory of human nature and the institution of government, which led him, in 1838, to renounce the parish church and refuse to pay its tax, in 1846 to renounce the State and refuse tribute to it, and in 1859 to come forward, first of all men, in public support of Brown and his Virginia campaign. This theory found frequent expression in his lectures. In 1846 he said: —

"Any man more right than his neighbors constitutes a majority of one already."

And again: —

"I know this well, that if one thousand, if one hundred, if ten men whom I could name, — if ten *honest* men only, — ay, if one honest man, *ceasing to hold slaves*, were actually to withdraw from this copartnership, and be locked up in the county jail therefor, it would be the abolition of slavery in America. Under a government which imprisons any unjustly, the true place for a just man is also a prison."

This sounded hollow then, but when that embodiment of American justice and mercy, John Brown, lay bleeding in a Virginia prison, a dozen years later, the significance of Thoreau's words began to be seen; and when a few years after our countrymen were dying by hundreds of thousands to complete what Brown, with his single life, had begun, the whole truth, as Thoreau had seen it, flashed in the eyes of the nation.

In this same essay of 1846, on "Civil Disobedience," the ultimate truth concerning government is stated in a passage which also does justice to Daniel Webster, our "logic-fencer and parliamentary Hercules," as Carlyle called him in a letter to Emerson in 1839. Thoreau said: —

"Statesmen and legislators, standing so completely within the institution (of government) never distinctly and nakedly behold it. They speak of moving society, but have no resting-place without it. They are wont to forget that the world is not governed by policy and expediency. Webster never goes behind government, and so cannot speak with authority about it. His words are wisdom to those legislators who contemplate no essential reform in the existing government; but for thinkers, and those who legislate for all time, he never once glances at the subject. Yet compared with the cheap professions of most reformers, and the still cheaper wisdom and eloquence of politicians in general, his are almost the only sensible and valuable words, and we thank heaven for him. Comparatively, he is always strong, original, and, above all, practical; still his quality is not wisdom, but prudence. Truth is always in harmony with herself, and is not concerned chiefly to reveal the justice that may consist with wrong-doing. For eighteen hundred years the New Testament has been written; yet where is the legislator who has wisdom and practical talent enough to avail himself of the light which it sheds on the science of government?"

Such a legislator, proclaiming his law

from the scaffold, at last appeared in John Brown: —

"I see a book kissed here which I suppose to be the Bible, or at least the New Testament. That teaches me that 'whatsoever I would that men should do unto me, I should do even so to them.' It teaches me further to 'remember them that are in bonds as bound with them.' I endeavored to act up to that instruction. I say that I am yet too young to understand that God is any respecter of persons. I believe that, to have interfered as I have done in behalf of His despised poor, was not wrong, but right."

Before these simple words of Brown, down went Webster and all his industry in behalf of the "compromises of the Constitution." When Thoreau heard them, and saw the matchless behavior of his noble old friend, he recognized the hour and the man.

"For once," he cried in the church-vestry at Concord, "we are lifted into the region of truth and manhood. No man, in America, has ever stood up so persistently and effectively for the dignity of human nature; knowing himself for a man, and the equal of any and all governments. The only government that I recognize, — and it matters not how few are at the head of it, or how small its army, — is that power which establishes justice in the land."

Words like these have proved immortal when spoken in the cell of Socrates, and they lose none of their vitality, coming from the Concord philosopher.

The weakness of Webster was in his moral principles ; he could not resist temptation; could not keep out of debt; could not avoid those obligations which the admiration or the selfishness of his friends forced upon him, and which left him, in his old age, neither independence nor gratitude. Thoreau's strength was in his moral nature, and in his obstinate refusal to mortgage himself, his time, or his opinions, even to the State or the Church. The haughtiness of his independence kept him from a thousand temptations that beset men of less courage and self-denial.

CHAPTER XIII.

LIFE, DEATH, AND IMMORTALITY.

THE life of Thoreau naturally divides itself into three parts: his Apprenticeship, from birth to the summer of 1837, when he left Harvard College; his Journey-work (Wanderjahre) from 1837 to 1849, when he appeared as an author, with his first book; and his Mastership, — not of a college, a merchantman, or a mechanic art, but of the trade and mystery of writing. He had aspired to live and study and practice, so that he could write — to use his own words — "sentences which suggest far more than they say, which have an atmosphere about them, which do not report an old, but make a new impression." To frame such sentences as these, he said, "as durable as a Roman aqueduct," was the art of writing coveted by him; "sentences which are expressive, towards which so many volumes, so much life went; which lie like boulders on the page, up and down or across, — not mere repetition, but creation, and which a man might sell his ground or cattle to build." It was this thirst for final and concentrated expression, and not love of fame, or "literary aspirations," as poor Greeley put it, which urged him on to write. For printing he cared little, — and few authors since Shakespeare have been less anxious to publish what they wrote. Of the seven volumes of his works yet printed, and as many more which may be published some day, only two, "The Week" and "Walden," appeared in his lifetime, — though the material for two more had been scattered about in forgotten magazines and newspapers, for his friends to collect after his death. Of his first works (and some of his best) it could be said, as Thomas Wharton said, in 1781, of his friend Gray's verses, "I yet reflect with pain upon the cool reception which those noble odes, 'The Progress of Poetry' and 'The Bard' met with at their first publication; it appeared there were not twenty people in England who liked them." This disturbed Thoreau's friends, but not himself; he rather rejoiced in the slow sale of his first book; and when the balance of the edition,—more than seven hundred copies out of one thousand,—came back upon his hands unsold in 1855, or thereabout, he told me with glee that he had made an addition of seven hundred volumes to his library, and all of his own composition. "O solitude, obscurity, meanness!" he exclaims in 1856 to his friend Blake, "I never triumph so as when I have the least success in my neighbors' eyes." Of course, pride had something to do with this; "it was a wild stock of pride," as Burke said of Lord Keppel, "on which the tenderest of all hearts had grafted the milder virtues." Both pride and piety led him to write,—

> "Fame cannot tempt the bard
> Who 's famous with his God,
> Nor laurel him reward
> Who has his Maker's nod."

Though often ranked as an unbeliever, and too scornful in some of his expressions concerning the religion of other men, Thoreau was in truth deeply religious. Sincerity and devotion were his most marked traits; and both are seen in his verses from the same poem ("Inspiration") so often quoted: —

"I will then trust the love untold
Which not my worth or want hath bought, —
Which wooed me young and wooes me old,
And to this evening hath me brought."

Thoreau's business in life was observation, thought, and writing, to which last, reading was essential. He read much, but studied more; nor was his reading that indiscriminate, miscellaneous perusal of everything printed, which has become the vice of this age. He read books of travel, scientific books, authors of original merit, but few newspapers, of which he had a very poor opinion. "Read not the 'Times,' read the Eternities," he said. Nor did he admire the magazines, or their editors, greatly. He quarreled with "Putnam's Magazine," in 1853–54, and in 1858, after yielding to the suggestion of Mr. Emerson, that he should contribute to the "Atlantic," in consequence of a dispute with Mr. Lowell, its editor, about the omission of a sentence in one of his articles, he published no more in that magazine until the year of his death (1862), when Mr. Fields obtained from him some of his choicest manuscripts. He spent the last months of his life in revising these, and they continued to appear for some years after his death. Those which have since been published in the "Atlantic" are passages from his journals, selected by his friend Blake, who now has the custody of his manuscripts. These consist chiefly of his journals in thirty volumes, many parts of which have already been printed, either by Thoreau himself, by his sister Sophia, or his friend Channing, who, in 1873, published a life of Thoreau, containing many extracts from the journals, which had never before been printed. When we speak of his works, we should include Mr. Channing's book also, half of which, at least, is from Thoreau's pen.

His method in writing was peculiarly his own, though it bore some external resemblance to that of his friends, Emerson and Alcott. Like them he early began to keep a journal, which became both diary and commonplace book. But while they noted down the thoughts which occurred to them, without premeditation or consecutive arrangement, Thoreau made studies and observations for his journal as carefully and habitually as he noted the angles and distances in surveying a Concord farm. In all his daily walks and distant journeys, he took notes on the spot of what occurred to him, and these, often very brief and symbolic, he carefully wrote out, as soon as he could get time, in his diary, not classified by topics, but just as they had come to him. To these he added his daily meditations, sometimes expressed in verse, especially in the years between 1837 and 1850, but generally in close and pertinent prose. Many details are found in his diaries, but not such as are common in the diaries of other men, — not trivial but significant details. From these daily entries he made up his essays, his lectures, and his volumes; all being slowly, and with much deliberation and revision, brought into the form in which he gave them to the public. After that he scarcely changed them at all; they had received the last imprint of his mind, and he allowed them to stand and speak for themselves. But before printing, they underwent constant change, by addition, erasure, transposition, correction, and combination. A given lecture might be two years, or twenty years in preparation; or it might be, like his defense of John Brown, copied with little change from the pages of his diary for the fortnight previous. But that was an exceptional case; and Thoreau was stirred and quickened by the campaign and capture of Brown, as perhaps he had never been before.

"The thought of that man's position and fate," he said, "is spoiling many a man's day here at the North for other thinking. If any one who has seen John Brown in Concord, can pursue successfully any other train of thought, I do not know what he is made of. If there is any such who gets his usual allowance of sleep, I will warrant him to fatten easily under any circumstances which do not touch his body or purse. I put a piece of paper and a pencil under my pillow, and when I could not sleep, I wrote in the dark. I was so absorbed in him as to be surprised whenever I detected the routine of the natural world surviving still, or met persons going about their affairs indifferent."

The fact that Thoreau noted down his thoughts by night as well as by day, appear also from an entry in one of his journals, where he is describing the coming on of day, as witnessed by him at the close of a September night in Concord. "Some bird flies over," he writes, "making a noise like the barking of a puppy (it was a cuckoo). It is yet so dark that I have dropped my pencil and cannot find it." No writer of modern times, in fact, was so much awake and abroad at night, or has described better the phenomena of darkness and of moonlight.

It is interesting to note some dates and incidents concerning a few of Thoreau's essays. The celebrated chapter on "Friendship," in the "Week," was written in the winter of 1847–48, soon after he left Walden, and while he was a member of Mr. Emerson's household during the absence of his friend in Europe. On the 13th of January, 1848, Mr. Alcott notes in his diary: —

"Henry Thoreau came in after my hours with the children, and we had a good deal of talk on the modes of popular influence. He read me a manuscript essay of his on 'Friendship,' which he has just written, and which I thought superior to anything I had heard."

To the same period or a little later belong those verses called "The Departure," which declare, under a similitude, Thoreau's relations with one family of his friends.

In 1843, when he first met Henry James, Lucretia Mott, and others who have since been famous, in the pleasant seclusion of Staten Island, he wrote a translation of the "Seven Against Thebes," which has never been printed, some translations from Pindar, printed in the "Dial," in 1844, and two articles for the New York "Democratic Review," called "Paradise to be Regained," and "The Landlord."

Thoreau left "a vast amount of manuscript," in the words of his sister, who was his literary executor until her death in 1876, when she committed her trust to his Worcester friend, Mr. Harrison Blake. She was aided in the revision and publication of the "Excursions," "Maine Woods," "Letters," and other volumes which she issued from 1862 to 1866, by Mr. Emerson, Mr. Channing, and other friends, — Mr. Emerson having undertaken that selection of letters and poems from his mass of correspondence and his preserved verses, which appeared in 1865. His purpose, as he said to Miss Thoreau, was to exhibit in that volume "a most perfect piece of stoicism," and he fancied that she had "marred his classic statue" by inserting some tokens of natural affection which the domestic letters showed. Miss Thoreau said that "it did not seem quite honest to Henry" to leave out such passages; Mr. Fields, the publisher, agreed with her, and a few of them were retained. His correspondence, as a whole, is much more affectionate, and less pugnacious than would appear from the published volume. He was fond of dispute, but those who knew him best loved him most.

Of his last illness his sister said: —

"It was not possible to be sad in his presence. No shadow of gloom attaches to anything in my mind connected with my precious brother. He has done much to strengthen the faith of his friends. Henry's whole life impresses me as a grand miracle."

Walking once with Mr. Alcott, soon after he passed his eightieth birth day, as we faced the lovely western sky in December, the old Pythagorean said, "I always think of Thoreau when I look at a sunset;" and

I then remembered it was at that hour Thoreau usually walked along the village street, under the arch of trees, with the sunset sky seen through their branches. "He said to me in his last illness," added Alcott, 'I shall leave the world without a regret,' — that was the saying either of a grand egotist or of a deeply religious soul." Thoreau was both, and both his egotism and his devotion offended many of those who met him. His aversion to the companionship of men was partly religious — a fondness for the inward life — and partly egotism and scorn for frivolity.

"Emerson says his life is so unprofitable and shabby for the most part," writes Thoreau in 1854, "that he is driven to all sorts of resources, — and among the rest to men. I tell him we differ only in our resources: mine is to get away from men. They very rarely affect me as grand or beautiful; but I know that there is a sunrise and a sunset every day. I have seen more men than usual lately; and well as I was acquainted with one, I am surprised to find what vulgar fellows they are."

In 1859 he wrote to Mr. Blake: —

"I have lately got back to that glorious society called Solitude, where we meet our friends continually, and can imagine the outside world also to be peopled. Yet some of my acquaintance would fain hustle me into the almshouse for *the sake of society;* as if I were pining for that diet, when I seem to myself a most befriended man, and find constant employment. However, they do not believe a word I say. They have got a club, the handle of which is in the Parker House, at Boston, and with this they beat me from time to time, expecting to make me tender, or minced meat, and so fit for a club to dine off. The doctors are all agreed that I am suffering for want of society. Was never a case like it! First, I did not know that I was suffering at all. Secondly, as an Irishman might say, I had thought it was indigestion of the society I got."

Yet Thoreau knew the value of society, and avoided it oftentimes only because he was too busy. To his friend Ricketson, who reproached him for ceasing to answer letters, he wrote in November, 1860, just before he took the fatal cold that terminated in consumption and ended his life prematurely: —

"FRIEND RICKETSON, — You know that I never promised to correspond with you, and so, when I do, I do more than I promised. Such are my pursuits and habits, that I rarely go abroad; and it is quite a habit with me to decline invitations to do so. Not that I could not enjoy such visits, if I were not otherwise occupied. I have enjoyed very much my visits to you, and my rides in your neighborhood, and am sorry that I cannot enjoy such things oftener; but life is short, and there are other things also to be done. I admit that you are more social than I am, and more attentive to 'the common courtesies of life;' but this is partly for the reason that you have fewer or less exacting private pursuits. Not to have written a note for a year is with me a very venial offense. I think I do not correspond with any one so often as once in six months. I have a faint recollection of your invitation referred to; but I suppose I had no new or particular reason for declining, and so made no new statement. I have felt that you would be glad to see me almost whenever I got ready to come; but I only offer myself as a rare visitor, and a still rarer correspondent. I am very busy, after my fashion, little as there is to show for it, and feel as if I could not spend many days nor dollars in traveling; for the shortest visit must have a fair margin to it, and the days thus affect the weeks, you know.

"Nevertheless, we cannot forego these luxuries altogether. Please remember me to your family. I have a very pleasant recollection of your fireside, and I trust that I shall revisit it; also of your shanty and the surrounding regions."

He did make a last visit to this friend in August, 1861, after his return from Minnesota, whither he went with young Horace Mann, in June. And it was to Mr. Ricketson that Sophia Thoreau, two weeks after her brother's death, wrote the following account of his last illness: —

"CONCORD, *May* 20, 1862.

"DEAR FRIEND, — Profound joy mingles with my grief. I feel as if something very beautiful had happened, — not death. Although Henry is with us no longer, yet the memory of his sweet and virtuous soul must ever cheer and comfort me. My heart is filled with praise to God for the gift of such a brother, and may I never distrust the love and wisdom of Him who made him, and who has now called him to labor in more glorious fields than earth affords!

"You ask for some particulars relating to Henry's illness. I feel like saying that Henry was never affected, never reached by it. I never before saw such a manifestation of the power of spirit over matter. Very often I have heard him tell his visitors that he enjoyed existence as well as ever. He remarked to me that there was as much comfort in perfect disease as in perfect health, the mind always conforming to the condition of the body. The thought of death, he said, could not begin to trouble him. His thoughts had entertained him all his life, and did still. When he had wakeful nights, he would ask me to arrange the furniture, so as to make fantastic shadows on the wall, and he wished his bed was in the form of a shell that he might curl up in it. He considered occupation as necessary for the sick as for those in health, and has accomplished a vast amount of labor during the past few months, in preparing some papers for the press. He did not cease to call for his manuscript till the last day of his life. During his long illness I never heard a murmur escape him, or the slightest wish expressed to remain with us. His perfect contentment was truly wonderful. None of his friends seemed to realize how very ill he was, so full of life and good cheer did he seem. One friend, as if by way of consolation, said to him, 'Well, Mr. Thoreau, we must all go.' Henry replied, 'When I was a very little boy, I learned that I must die, and I set that down, so, of course, I am not disappointed now. Death is as near to you as it is to me.'

"There is very much that I should like to write you about my precious brother had I time and strength. I wish you to know how very gentle, lovely, and submissive he was in all his ways. His little study bed was brought down into our front parlor, when he could no longer walk with our assistance, and every arrangement pleased him. The devotion of his friends was most rare and touching. His room was made fragrant by the gifts of flowers from young and old. Fruit of every kind which the season afforded, and game of all sorts, were sent him. It was really pathetic, the way in which the town was moved to minister to his comfort. Total strangers sent grateful messages, remembering the good he had done them. All this attention was fully appreciated and very gratifying to Henry. He would sometimes say, 'I should be ashamed to stay in this world after so much has been done for me. I could never repay my friends.' And they remembered him to the last. Only about two hours before he left us, Judge Hoar called with a bouquet of hyacinths fresh from his garden, which Henry smelt and said he liked, and a few minutes after he was gone another friend came with a dish of his favorite jelly. I can never be grateful enough for the gentle, easy exit which was granted him. At seven o'clock, Tuesday morning, he became restless, and desired to be moved. Dear Mother, aunt Louisa, and myself were with him. His self-possession did not forsake him. A little after eight he asked to be raised quite up. His breathing grew fainter and fainter, and without the slightest struggle, he left us at nine o'clock, — but not alone; our Heavenly Father was with us.

"Your last letter reached us by the evening mail on Monday. Henry asked me to read it to him, which I did. He enjoyed your letters, and felt disappointed not to see you again. Mr. Blake and Mr. Brown came twice to visit him, since January. They were present at his funeral, which took place in the church. Mr. Emerson read such an address as no other man could have done. It is a source of great satisfaction that one so gifted knew and loved my brother, and is prepared to speak such brave words about him at this time. The 'Atlantic Monthly' for July will contain Mr. Emerson's memories of Henry. I hope that you saw a notice of the services on Friday, written by Mr. Fields, in the 'Transcript.'

"Let me thank you for your very friendly letters. I trust we shall see you in Concord, Anniversary Week. It would give me pleasure to make the acquaintance of your family, of whom my brother has so often told me. If convenient, will you please bring the ambrotype of Henry which was taken last autumn in New Bedford. I am interested to see it. Mr. Channing will take the crayon likeness to Boston this week to secure some photographs. My intention was to apologize for not writing you at this time; but I must now trust to your generosity to pardon this hasty letter, written under a great pressure of cares and amidst frequent interruptions. My mother unites with me in very kind regards to your family.

"Yours truly, S. E. THOREAU."

To Parker Pillsbury, who would fain talk with Thoreau in this last winter concerning the next world, the reply was, "One world at a time." To a young friend (Myron Benton) he wrote a few weeks before death: —

"CONCORD, *March* 21, 1862.

"DEAR SIR, — I thank you for your very kind letter, which, ever since I received it, I have intended to answer before I died, however briefly. I am encouraged to know, that, so far as you are concerned, I have not written my books in vain. I was particularly gratified, some years ago, when one of my friends and neighbors said, 'I wish you would write another book — write it for me.' He is actually more familiar with what I have written than I am myself. I am pleased when you say that in 'The Week' you like especially 'those little snatches of poetry interspersed through the book;' for these, I suppose, are the least attractive to most readers. I have not been engaged in any particular work on Botany, or the like, though, if I were to live, I should have much to report on Natural History generally.

"You ask particularly after my health. I *suppose* that I have not many months to live; but, of course, I know nothing about it. I may add, that I am enjoying existence as much as ever, and regret nothing.

"Yours truly, HENRY D. THOREAU,
"By SOPHIA E. THOREAU."

"With an unfaltering trust in God's mercies," wrote Ellery Channing, "and never deserted by his good genius, he most bravely and unsparingly passed down the inclined plane of a terrible malady—pulmonary consumption; working steadily at the completing of his papers to his last hours, or so long as he could hold the pencil in his trembling fingers. Yet if he did get a little sleep to comfort him in this year's campaign of sleepless affliction, he was sure to interest those about him in his singular dreams, more than usually fantastic. He said once, that having got a few moments of repose, 'sleep seemed to hang round his bed in festoons.' He declared uniformly that he preferred to endure with a clear mind the worst penalties of suffering rather than be plunged in a turbid dream by narcotics. His patience was unfailing; assuredly he knew not aught save resignation; he did mightily cheer and console those whose strength was less. His every instant now, his least thought and work, sacredly belonged to them, dearer than his rapidly perishing life, whom he should so quickly leave behind."

Once or twice he shed tears. Upon hearing a wandering musician in the street playing some tune of his childhood he might never hear again, he wept, and said to his mother, "Give him some money for me!"

> "Northward he turneth through a little door,
> And scarce three steps, ere Music's golden tongue,
> Flattered to tears this aged man and poor;
> But no — already had his death-bell rung,
> The joys of all his life were said and sung."

He died on the 6th of May, 1862, and had a public funeral from the parish church a few days later. On his coffin his friend

Channing placed several inscriptions, among them this, "Hail to thee, O man! who hast come from the transitory place to the imperishable." This sentiment may stand as faintly marking Thoreau's deep, vital conviction of immortality, of which he never had entertained a doubt in his life. There was in his view of the world and its Maker no room for doubt; so that when he was once asked, superfluously, what he thought of a future world and its compensations, he replied, "Those were voluntaries I did not take," — having confined himself to the foreordained course of things. He is buried in the village cemetery, quaintly named "Sleepy Hollow," with his family and friends about him; one of whom, surviving him for a few years, said, as she looked upon his low head-stone on the hillside, "Concord is Henry's monument, covered with suitable inscriptions by his own hand."

INDEX.

Journalist and humanitarian FRANK B. SANBORN (1831-1917) was a prominent resident of Concord and became an intimate associate of Thoreau's. Working as John Brown's New England agent, he was responsible for introducing Thoreau to the abolitionist martyr. In addition, Sanborn was a founder in 1879 of the Concord School of Philosophy. His close involvement with the Concord Circle led him to write biographies not only of Thoreau, but also of Brown, Alcott, Emerson, and Hawthorne.

LEO MARX is William R. Kenan, Jr., Professor of American Cultural History at Massachusetts Institute of Technology. He is the author of *The Machine in the Garden: Technology and the Pastoral Ideal in America.*